FACSIMILE EDITION
OF
A
Practical Treatise
ON
PLANTING;
AND
The Management of
Woods and Coppices.

By S.H. *Esq.* M.R.I.A. *and*
Member of the Committee of Agriculture,
of the
DUBLIN SOCIETY,
FOREWORD
BY
THOMAS PAKENHAM

Published by
New Island
of
DUBLIN

Printed by
Dundalgan Press (W. Tempest) Ltd.,
DUNDALK, IRELAND
MMIII

SAMUEL HAYES
Practical Treatise on Trees
published 2003
by New Island
2 Brookside
Dundrum Road
Dublin 14
www.newisland.ie

Originally published as *A Practical Treatise on Planting and the Managment of Woods and Coppices* in 1794

Foreword ©2003 THOMAS PAKENHAM

ISBN 1 902602 94 3

Endpaper image: Avondale House and the demense by the river Avon. A watercolour by D. A. Beaufort, *c.* late 18th Century. Reproduced by kind permission of the Knight of Glin.

New Island gratefully acknowledges the support of The Irish Tree Society

Please note: Pagination of additional material at the beginning of this edition is indicated by uppercase roman numerals. All other numerals follow the pagination of the original edition.

All rights reserved. The material in this publication is protected by copyright law. Except as may be permitted by law, no part of the material may be reproduced (including by storage in a retrieval system) or transmitted in any form or by any means; adapted; rented or lent without the written permission of the copyright owners.

British Library Cataloguing in Publication Data. A CIP catalogue record for this book is available from the British Library.

Cover design by New Island
Printed in Ireland by Dundalgan Press.

New Island received financial assistance from
The Arts Council (An Chomhairle Ealaíon), Dublin, Ireland.

10 9 8 7 6 5 4 3 2 1

CONTENTS.

OF

FACSIMILE EDITION

FOREWORD BY THOMAS PAKENHAM

TEXT OF 1794

INDEX

Foreword.

by

THOMAS PAKENHAM

Chairman of the Irish Tree Society,
the sponsors of this new edition

If Samuel Hayes had not written his *Practical Treatise on Planting* he would have been almost completely lost in the shadows. As it is he remains an elusive figure.

We know some of the basic facts about him. He was born in 1743 and before he was thirty had inherited a 4,500-acre estate in County Wicklow beside a wild, rocky stretch of the Avonmore River. His father had called it by the prosaic name of Hayesville but Samuel Hayes thought he would do better. In 1770 he rechristened it Avondale, and built a house on the terrace above the river, a grey stone box in the neo-classical style, rather as James Wyatt would have designed it, but with gothic trefoils inlaid in the panels of the doors, and acorns cast in plaster dominating the hall. As far as we know he was his own architect. He must have been an unusually talented amateur: it's a calm, elegant house. Out in the demesne he planted trees with reckless abandon: native sessile oaks from local acorns, and six of the great European species that have naturalised in Ireland, beech and walnut, sycamore and sweet chestnut, common spruce and silver fir. With a handful of other patriotic enthusiasts he promoted the fashion for planting trees as both timber and ornament.

By profession he was a barrister – he was called to the Irish bar when he was twenty-four – and soon he found a wider stage for his ambitions. In 1783 he was elected MP for the borough of Wicklow and later served as member for the borough of Maryborough (the modern Portlaoise) and as Commissioner of Stamps. He was one of the Wicklow delegates to the Volunteer Convention of 1783 and a colonel of the self-styled 'Wicklow Foresters', a Volunteer regiment.

A decade later the government made him Lieutenant-Colonel of the Wicklow militia, an important post for an amateur soldier. He died in November 1795, only a year after he had published *A Practical Treatise on Planting*, leaving Avondale to his close friend (and mother's first cousin) Sir John Parnell. His plantations, and those of his Parnell successors, flourished like the proverbial bay tree. But I doubt whether Avondale would have become famous if Sir John had not turned out to be Charles Stewart Parnell's great-grandfather. Today Avondale is a national centre of forestry – and also a shrine to that doomed champion of Irish independence.

I'm afraid Samuel Hayes would have taken a dim view of his celebrated descendant. In his political career Hayes showed no sign of dissent, at least in politics, from the orthodoxies of the Protestant landed gentry. He came to the Irish House of Commons during what would come to be regarded as an all-too brief golden age. Only a year earlier, with ill-concealed sympathy for the American rebels, the Volunteers had paraded their guns in College Green. Then the Irish parliament in Dublin had extorted apparent independence from its British counterpart at Westminster. (In fact the British government still governed Ireland, as it still appointed the Irish executive.) Only a decade ahead loomed the abyss: the French Revolution and the seismic shocks that it spread across the whole of Europe. Within three years of Hayes' death, Ireland would have caught fire with ideas from republican France, and the 1798 Rebellion would engulf the counties around Avondale. By 1801 the Irish House of Commons would have vanished like a dream – swept away by the Act of Union with Great Britain, its elegant, domed chamber converted, appropriately, into a banking hall.

Who would have guessed this at the time Samuel Hayes sat on those well-padded benches? In many ways the eighteenth-century Irish House of Commons was like a parody of its British counterpart at Westminster. Its architecture was Palladian and neo-classical. But its most striking characteristic, as we would sense it today, was its unsavoury political smell. Two-thirds of the seats came from what were politely called 'closed boroughs' – meaning the rotten boroughs controlled by the great Protestant landed proprietors and the network of political small fry who depended on them. This was how things worked in the heyday of the 'Protestant ascendancy'. Interests were adjusted, wheels oiled, jobs and contracts and sinecures handed out, like toys or sweets, as a reward for voting for the government – that is, the Irish executive appointed by Britain.

We don't know how far Samuel Hayes had his fingers in the pie, but he had the right connections. His cousin, Sir John Parnell, was Chancellor of the Exchequer. One of his closest friends was John Foster, the 'Speaker' (but at times more like the leader) of the House of Commons. Hayes depended on them and their network for his seat in parliament and the lucrative post of Commissioner of Stamps – this was worth £500 a year. In return Hayes had much to offer Foster. As an amateur architect – he had already designed the courthouse in Monaghan – Hayes could help advise Foster in the hugely ambitious schemes then in progress for rebuilding Dublin. The two men also shared a passion for planting.

Hayes lacked the eloquence to be an effective public speaker, we are told by a contemporary critic. But 'his manner is certainly pleasing, open, free and unreserved, with a good deal of the honest candour of the country gentleman'. Hayes' most important stroke was in the in-fighting over the proposed extension to the House of Commons on College Green. Ten years earlier, in 1781, John Beresford, the Commissioner for the Revenue, had persuaded a young English architect, James Gandon, to come over from London to help re-build Dublin. Gandon's monumental buildings – the Custom House, Four Courts and extensions to the Houses of Parliament – still dominate the city today. But Gandon's plans for extending the House of Commons didn't appeal to Foster and other MPs: they preferred the design by their fellow MP, Samuel Hayes. In a private letter, later published in Gandon's biography, Hayes claimed that he, not Gandon, had designed the House of Commons façade that faces west. Could an unknown amateur's work really have been preferred to a distinguished professional's? Apparently it could and was. Go to the west side of what is now the Bank of Ireland in College Green. Look at the free-standing Ionic pediment. Hayes claimed he had designed it – and modern authorities support his claim.

In 1794, the year before his premature death (we

FOREWORD. xi

know nothing of the cause except that, three months before he died, he told one of the Parnells that he had 'the gout flying about me'), Hayes published in Dublin *A Practical Treatise on Planting*. It's as modest and unassuming as one would expect from a well-bred gentleman of that time. Its best-known feature is, deservedly, the fourteen delightful vignettes etched on copper and used for the title page, the tail pieces and the text in general. In fact the book has seventeen engravings, as three of the designs are used twice. Scholars usually refer to these illustrations as the work of William Esdall, a professional draughtsman and engraver in Dublin known for his elegant illustrations for books and periodicals. Esdall was certainly the engraver in this case but why give Esdall the credit for the *drawing*? I believe that Hayes himself was responsible.

Consider the evidence. We know that Hayes was, like many eighteenth-century men of taste, an amateur artist as well as an amateur architect. (One absentee magnate of Wicklow, Lord Fitzwilliam, was told by his steward about 'Mr. Hayes' who 'draws very well'. And there are various topographical drawings attributed to Hayes.) A careful look at *A Practical Treatise* gives one two reasons for believing that Hayes did the original drawings. First, Esdall doesn't claim to have been any more than the engraver. His signature ('*Esdall sculpsit*') appears on four of the etchings; the other ten are anonymous. By contrast, we know that Hayes himself drew one of the finest ('*S.H. del*' appears on the great ash of Leix on page 105) and 'designed' another (the Gothick woodhouse on page 67). Second, the fourteen vignettes are not mere embellishments. Most of them relate directly to the text. They illustrate such subjects as the design of pruning hooks, clippers, rustic fencing, techniques for felling oak and the heavy machinery needed to transplant big trees – unexpected subjects for an artist, unless he was himself the author.

We know little enough of how the book came to be written. Hayes tells us simply that 'several respectable members of the Dublin Society' (today the Royal Dublin Society) – and we may presume that his patrons, Foster and Parnell, were foremost among them – had talked him into writing a practical guidebook on trees to encourage their planting and correct management. Hayes was *the* acknowledged authority. He had been elected to the fifteen-strong Committee of Agriculture of the Dublin Society (which had paid out £1,220.11 in grants for the propagation and sale of trees in 1783 – 1791), was a member of the prestigious Royal Irish Academy and was the MP who had introduced a Bill for encouraging tenants to fence in their woodland to protect it from cattle.

The scope of the book, he tells us, was at first to be strictly practical – as you would guess from the title. It was to be an Irish do-it-yourself guide to two technical subjects: how to plant trees; and how to manage woods for timber (that is, planking wood) and coppices for small wood. This was more ambitious than it sounds. In fact this was to be Ireland's first *book* on trees. (An anonymous pamphlet, *Some Hints on Planting*, was published in Newry, County Down in 1773. Its author seems to have been either a local magnate, Lord Clermont, or his brother, James Fortescue. Both were friends of Hayes'.) No one in the country had yet attempted to follow in the footsteps of British gurus such as Philip Miller, the famous gardener at Chelsea, or Sir James Justice, the Scottish planter. But Hayes decided to go one better than these and other British predecessors. Teaching people how to plant trees and how to manage them, he explains, is one thing. To make them *love* them – to inspire them with 'the cause of planting, or preserving of timber', as he puts it – is quite another. So the second part of the book takes up these broader themes. He gives us a *tour d'horizon* of the remarkable trees in Ireland at the end of the eighteenth century. It's a dazzling and unique performance. Inevitably, almost all of these great trees are now long dead, and – but for Samuel Hayes – would have vanished without trace.

Does Hayes succeed in his task? Some people, he says, will find the book too 'circumstantial' – too full of technical detail – others will grumble that it omits their favourite trees. To the latter he offers his apologies, elegantly expressed. 'To those who may suppose I have despised their groves, and slighted their dryads ... I assure them that *want of time* ... has been the sole cause of this apparent neglect.' (We can say the same today, in the Irish Tree Society, when we unwittingly slight people's dryads.) But Hayes defends himself from the accusation that he's overreached himself. He cites the precedent of John Evelyn, Charles II's minister, whose celebrated book on trees, *Sylva*, sounded a call to patriotic Englishmen to plant trees which would one day become a vital resource for the British Navy. Hayes, too, sees this as a 'disinterested and patriotic' duty for his country-men. The call has a resonance in the age of global warming – even if British and Irish ships, fortunately for the trees, no longer depend on oak for their planking.

How does Hayes' book in general compare with its British counterparts? I'm struck by the modern ring of much of the practical advice in the initial sections. Clearly Hayes was a 'hands-on' planter. You can imagine him pottering about in his tree-nursery, a wide-brimmed hat on his head and a tailcoat below (like the men in his drawings), pruning up two-year-olds ready to transplant to the woods. He recommended creating a pyramidal shape in a young beech or oak before planting it out. But many British experts favoured sowing tree seeds, acorns and beech mast directly in the woods. Hayes denounced this practice – at least if applied to Ireland. There were far too many weeds and pests waiting to overwhelm the young seedling. Better start off your trees in a proper tree nursery where you can give the youngsters the best start in life. On the other hand Hayes was not afraid to regenerate new trees from old, using the stool-shoots from the stumps of veterans deliberately felled or blown down in storms. We should pay attention to Hayes' short cut. It still works admirably today, yet has been largely ignored

In the second part of the book, Hayes sets off enthusiastically on his *tour d'horizon* of remarkable trees. He concentrates at first on the trees in the parts of Ireland that he knew best: Wicklow and County Dublin. Perhaps it should be no surprise (for tree planting depends on generations of tree lovers) that his champions grow in the same great demesnes and gardens as give shelter to the champions of today. He describes Weymouth pine at Avondale, oaks at Shillelagh and Coolattin, silver firs at Mount Usher, beech at Shelton Abbey and so on. Shelton Abbey is especially interesting because Hayes tells us that this was the first demesne where beech was planted in Ireland, and was used as a seed source for other parts of the country. Botanists recognise that, about two thousand years ago, beech was native merely to southern England and other temperate regions of Europe. Then, part naturally, part with human assistance, it gradually spread far beyond that range, and became naturalised in much of Europe including the whole of Britain and Ireland. Hayes noticed the way the beech seems particularly well suited to Ireland. (By contrast, some modern ecologists advocate a kind of ethnic cleansing in which naturalised species, such as beech, are systematically hunted down and destroyed.) Sadly, the beech at Avondale that Hayes thought would be almost immortal – and there were few beech in Ireland more than two hundred years old in Hayes' time – have proved relatively short-lived. The young tree near the lawn that he knew when he was a boy crumbled into dust more than thirty years ago.

But a few trees that Hayes knew when he was young are still there to greet us today. Go down the River Avon and you will find two of the largest silver firs in Europe. I think they must have been planted by Hayes. So too the huge sweet chestnut close to the house and the twisted old oak below the lawn. Of course Avondale is also teeming with the descendants of the oak and beech and sycamore planted by Hayes. In 1794 someone wrote a purple passage about the view from the lawn. 'On the back of the house the ground in some parts slopes down with a gentle declivity, in other falls in steep and abrupt precipices, covered with ancient oaks, the roots of many of which are a hundred feet perpendicular over the topmost summit of others.' I think you would still recognise the view today.

His trees and his *Practical Treatise* are his most eloquent monuments. Eleven years after his death, a marble slab on the wall of the local church, St Saviour's at Rathdrum, was erected by a comrade in arms from the Rathdrum yeomanry, anxious to rescue 'from oblivion the respected Name of his friend':

>'Sacred to the Memory of
>SAMUEL HAYES
>of Avondale in this County, Esq.
>Member of Parliament
>for the Town of Maryborough,
>formerly Colonel of the Volunteer
>Regiment
>of Wicklow Foresters
>afterwards Lieutenant-Colonel of the
>Wicklow Militia,
>Who died on the 28th of November

1795,
Aged 52,
And is interred in the adjoining
Cemetery.

In his private Life, he was most
amiable,
In his Public, Active and loyal,
By his refined Taste he embellished
Nature ...'

An index by Thomas Pakenham appears on pages
191–200

Sources

Printed:

Brett, C.E.B. *Court Houses and Market Houses of the Province of Ulster*, U.A.H.S., 1973, pp. 94 (illustration), 96–97.

Johnston-Liik, Edith Mary (ed.) *History of the Irish Parliament 1692–1800*, vol. IV, Ulster Historical Foundation, 2002, pp. 388–389.

McCracken, Eileen 'Samuel Hayes of Avondale' in *Irish Forestry*, XX, pp. 38–41.

McParland, Edward *James Gandon*, London, 1985, pp. 84–87.

Mulvany, T.J. *The Life of James Gandon*, London, 1846, pp. 112–118.

Ray, Desmond *Dictionary of British and Irish Botanists and Horticulturalists*, London, 1994.

Unpublished:

Fitzwilliam Papers, Sheffield Library, Sheffield.

Parnell (Congleton) Papers, Southampton University, Southampton.

Irish Architectural Archive, Merrion Square, Dublin (Biographical Index of Irish Architects compiled by Ann Martha Rowan).

A Practical Treatise
ON
PLANTING;
AND
The Management of
Woods and Coppices.

By S. H. *Esq.* M.R.I.A. *and*
Member of the Committee of Agriculture,
of the
DUBLIN SOCIETY,
&c. &c.

DUBLIN,
Printed by Wm Sleater Dame Street
Printer to the Dublin Society;
And Sold by Allen & West,
N.º 15, PATERNOSTER ROW, LONDON.
MDCCXCIV.

THE FOLLOWING

PRACTICAL ESSAY

ON

PLANTING,

AND THE MANAGEMENT OF

WOODS AND COPPICES,

IS DEDICATED WITH GREAT REGARD,

TO THE RIGHT HONORABLE AND HONORABLE

The Dublin Society

FOR THE IMPROVEMENT OF

HUSBANDRY,

AND OTHER

USEFUL ARTS.

By their most obedient
And faithful Associate,

S. H.

Avondale, May 1794.

PREFACE.

WHEN in consequence of the wishes of several respectable Members of the *Dublin Society*, expressed in terms too flattering, not to ensure an immediate compliance, I undertook to give to the public a Short Practical Treatise on *Planting, and the Management of Woods*, it occurred to me at the moment, that I could not better fulfil the first part of my engagement, than by making a selection of such passages in the most approved writers on the subject as appeared best calculated for the soil and climate of this country; studying at the same time, to reconcile as much as lay in my power, that diversity of opinion, which on many occasions seems more likely to *distract* than *assist* the inexperienced Planter.

They

They have all propofed for their object the moft fpeedy and effectual method of *raifing timber;* but differ fo widely in the *means*, that *Miller* and Sir *James Juftice* advife the fowing of tree feeds on the ground where the trees are intended to remain; *Kenedy*, *Fortefcue*, and fome others, recommend planting out at once from the *feed-bed;* whilft *Boutcher* on the other hand, contends for frequent *tranfplantation*, even where trees have arrived to the height of twenty feet; and afferts, that in certain inftances, none, but fuch as have been thus managed, can be expected to fucceed.

The following Effay, it is hoped, may, in a great meafure reconcile thefe feeming contradictions, and point out, where the precepts of each author may be followed to moft advantage, by adapting them to thofe circumftances of foil and fituation, for which they

appear

PREFACE. vii

appear to have been originally defigned.

In the execution of this part of the
work, where I have fully approved of
the directions of the author, I have generally given them in his own words;
what may be wanting in point of ftile,
is often made up by fimplicity and a
fort of technical language, beft calculated in general, to convey information
to thofe, for whofe ufe it is principally
intended.——Where I have ventured to
differ in fome articles relative to *planting*,
from authors of eftablifhed reputation,
and through the *whole* of that part,
which treats of the *management of woods
and coppices*, I have written either from
my own experience, founded on confiderable practice, or from the communication of particular friends, amongft
whom, I may with truth affert, that
I can number thofe, who are not only as
fkilful Arborifts and extenfive Planters
as any in the kingdom; but at the fame
time,

time, are amongst the best informed in general, in every art and science, which can improve their country, or meliorate the state of its inhabitants.

To these two principal divisions of my subject, I have added a *third;* containing such instances as I have been enabled in the time to procure, of the magnitude and value to which certain trees have arrived in this kingdom, and of the rapid progress which others have made towards repaying the expence and attention of the Planter; the *one* being designed to inculcate the advantages resulting from the proper management and *preservation of our woods,* and the *other*, as the best inducement to the *extension of our plantations.*

If I have carried this enquiry to rather a greater length than was at first intended, I flatter myself, it will be found to contain some interesting circumstances, which may induce those to

peruse

peruse a work, which they would not have once thought of looking into, had I confined myself to the *didactic* part alone; and if thus I shall add but an individual to the cause of *planting*, or *preserving* of timber, I shall consider neither my own time nor that of my reader as unprofitably employed.

How far this attempt may conduce to carry into effect, the purposes for which it was undertaken, a future day can alone determine; in the mean time, I have the satisfaction of thinking, that in giving it, such as it is, to the public, I avoid the imputation of being an idle Member of a SOCIETY of GENTLEMEN distinguished for many years, by their patriotic and disinterested exertions in the advancement of the Arts, Manufactures, and the Agriculture of their country.

CONTENTS.

                              Page

Directions for enclosing Ground,   1 *to* 5

Observations on the Nursery,   5 *to* 18

Pruning of Trees at the Time of transplanting,   18 *to* 25

Directions for planting, suited to the various Soils and Situations,   28 *to* 67

On pruning and the Management of Woods,   69 *to* 104

Value of Oak at different Periods of its Growth,   72 *to* 79 & 172

Great Loss from the premature felling of Timber,   75 *to* 91

Advantages resulting from the Law in favour of Tenants planting, or inclosing young Wood,   93

a   *Bounty*

CONTENTS.

	Page
Bounty granted to such Tenants on determinable Leases, by the Dublin Society,	185
Directions for making the Dutch Wax, for grafting or covering the Wounds of Trees,	101
Directions for making Mr Forsythe's *Composition for curing Injuries in Fruit and Forest Trees,*	102
The Magnitude and Value of several Trees in Ireland,	105 to 157
Extraordinary Size and great Value of some Trees now standing in England,	125, 6, 7
Rapid Growth of Trees in particular Situations in Ireland,	153 to 180
Bounties paid by the Dublin Society, from the Year 1783 *to the Year* 1791, *on the Propagation and Sale of Timber Trees, Number of Trees sold,* &c *and the progressive Improvement of the country in consequence of these Bounties,*	183

PRACTICAL TREATISE
On PLANTING, &c.

I shall follow the ingenious and experienced author of *Hints on Planting*, in prefacing all I mean to say on the subject, by calling the attention of the Plan er in the first instance to the security of his enclosure. In vain he plants, if cattle can get amongst his young trees; they totally destroy such as are within their reach, and materially injure those of a more advanced growth.

Where we have security alone in view, and a lime and stone wall would not present a disagreeable object, it is certainly the best fence possible; a dry stone-wall, with the upper course laid in mortar, and covered with two rows of turf or sods, the grass side of one turned under, the other upwards, makes a good fence; but as I have found by experience that shelter is in most situations more essential to young plantations than any other

other circumstance, I recommend a stone-faced ditch; the stones to be laid in mortar, or well bedded with sods to prevent the effect of the air on the roots of the quicks, which should be three year old white-thorn, or crab-tree, laid over the first row of stones. The trench to be sunk about five feet, and made six or seven feet wide. If the ground be inclinable to moisture, sallow cuttings may be planted, as top-sets, crossing each other, so as to form a sort of net-work; these will soon make an impenetrable fence, and afford great shelter.— Hornbeam is used for this purpose in Germany; the branches having a little of the bark taken off where they cross each other, and being tied in the form desired, soon grow together, into a continued pallisade—in grounds too poor to support the above, cuttings of elder may be planted in the same manner, and common broom, or French furz-seed, may be sown in a little drill at the back, which will afford useful shelter in a very short time—when quicks are planted in the face of the ditch, it is an excellent method to insert young holly plants at about four feet distance in May or June following; I should also wish to recommend a more

frequent

frequent use of the crab than is generally practiced; by no means for the purpose of grafting, or suffering them to bear fruit, as that would, in this situation have a direct tendency to defeat the purpose of planting them: but as a strong growing, vigorous plant in many soils, where the white thorn grows but poorly, and especially in a wet strong clay, or in a moor over white gravel, both of which soils seem ill-adapted to the growth of the white thorn; which ever plant is found to answer it, will be improved by clipping the breast and tapering up the hedge, but suffering the top to grow for a confiderable time without shortening. Lord Kaims (who feems to leave nothing uninvestigated, from the formation of man to the growth of a crab) in his Gentleman's Farmer, inveighs strongly against the practice of clipping the tops of young hedges, and afferts, with reason, founded, I can aver, on experience, that trees so used, never acquire equal strength of stem and vigorous growth with those suffered to run for a confiderable time without stopping; as may be feen in those hedges where fome thorns have been preferved as *standards*, he therefore

therefore advises our leaving the hedge at full liberty at top, until the stems are about two inches thick, and then to cut them at the height of three or four feet, keeping it afterwards in a taper form, which admits the access of sun and rain to every part.—Anderson in his Treatise on Agriculture, agrees with Lord Kaims; but instead of only clipping the first shoots, recommends shortening all the side ones still as they put out, by which strong spurs are formed, which soon meeting and crossing each other, make a most impenetrable and lasting fence: but this practice would be difficult to adopt in a great extent of hedging.—The English method of plashing, undoubtedly shortens the duration of the fence: where we can wait for the natural strong growth recommended by Lord Kaims and Mr. Anderson, there cannot be a more durable and effective enclosure: but in many situations it may be adviseable that the quicks should be shortened when about three feet high, both to prevent the hedges growing thin at bottom; and to take away the temptation of cutting them for flails or walking sticks.—Where hedging is plenty, a

small

small stake-hedge improves the fence, whilst the young quicks are growing; but I have generally obferved, that few things in hufbandry are worfe executed in Ireland than dead hedges: the ftakes are left irregular, and awkwardly long above the hedge, which affords an opportunity to hedge-breakers to pull them out with facility, and the wattling or lacing which is worked through the ftakes is laid *too flat;* confequently holds water and rots in a very fhort time: the pofition of the lacing fhould be at an angle of forty-five degrees, and the whole made firm and bound down by long twifted binders wrought like the upper rim of a bafket; the ftakes fhould then be driven down again and fhortened with a floping cut, about four inches over the binding; a ftake-hedge made as above, may laft five years very well.

Having thus fecured his ground, the Planter fhould turn his thoughts to his nurfery, or other means of procuring his ftock of plants; and here variety of fituations and foils, with which the different writers on this fubject have been converfant, has caufed fuch a diverfity of opinions,

opinions, that the Planter has need of exerting his judgment in deciding which he may adopt with the greatest probability of success.

However respectable the authority of those writers who have recommended the sowing tree seeds, where they are to remain, as the best means of raising valuable timber,—I would by no means have the Planter pursue their advice in a country so much inclined to the growth of grafs and strong weeds, as is generally the case in most parts of Ireland.—I am confident, from my own experience, that the decided opinions of Miller, and Sir James Justice, in favour of the above practice, has retarded the growth of many plantations in this kingdom, and deadened the ardour of many a Planter, whose trees would long since have afforded, not only ornament and shelter, but profit, had he taken either Fortescue or Boutcher for his guide—though, I allow at the same time, that there may be some situations where partial sowing will be found advantageous—the Planter should have a nursery of his own, if he can command a light mellow soil, on which

most

moſt kind of trees may be raiſed to advantage.

For every ſpecies of fir, I think there can be no better proceſs than that recommended by the Author of the Treatiſe on the Pinus Silveſtris, by which he means the Scotch Fir, though properly ſpeaking, it is the Pinaſter.

He directs the ſeed to be ſown on beds three feet broad, about as thick as onions, very lightly covered with earth, not above half an inch thick at *moſt*.—The beſt way to aſcertain that thickneſs is, after the bed has been made ſmooth with the back of a ſpade and the ſeed ſown, to lay on the bed a few ſmall laths, half an inch thick, and then to ſift on earth with a fine wire riddle, 'till it comes to the top of the laths.—The whole may then be ſmoothed and dreſſed as uſual.

If the weather be dry, water the ſeeds gently with a fine roſe.—The ground of the beds ſhould be rich, but not newly dunged, ſhould be rather a light than a ſtiff ſoil, by no means

expoſed

exposed to the sun, nor yet under the drip of trees, and open at least to the North.

When the plants spring they bring up their seeds on their tops, which attract all the birds in the neighbourhood, who would, if not prevented, devour them entirely.—The best way, is to cover the bed with a close mashed net.—Nothing farther need be done till the beginning of winter, unless weeding the beds now and then; to prevent the little plants from being forced out of the ground by the frost, it is good to sift a quantity of *saw-dust*, shellings of meal, turf-mould, sand, or ashes, merely a sufficiency to insinuate itself amongst the young plants, about twelve thousand of which may be expected from the pound of the Scots fir seed.—The small twigs or boughs of timber trees, such as elm or beech, spread thick but lightly on the beds, are known to keep out frost better than more solid substances; the method above recommended of sowing fir seeds on beds of no greater breadth than three feet, will be found the most advantageous for all sorts of tree seeds.—They are kept clear of weeds without injuring the
young

young plants, and in taking them up for transplantation, the whole roots may be raised together from the bed by two spades opposite each other, without injuring a single fibre; the quantity also which will stand on such beds, if properly sown, will not be too great so as to mildew, or cause the seedling plants to be too much drawn up: On the other hand, I have found single drills, though recommended by many books on the subject of planting, to be liable to great failures, from being too much exposed to sun, wind, and cold.—I would, therefore, sow all tree seeds on small beds, and if they come up too thick, thin them with discretion the first year.—Those which are thus taken out, may be pricked into other beds, and will in two years be fit for planting out.

The seeds should be covered with fine mould, pretty much in proportion to their size, the smallest requiring about half an inch, and the largest, such as the walnut and chesnut, from two to three inches, according to the nature of the soil; but if it were not from an apprehension of injury from mice, birds, &c. I think it much

better

better to give rather a light than a deep covering.—It is more agreeable to the procefs of Nature, where the acorn is often found, vegetating with vigour on the furface of the ground, and by this means, more foil is afforded under the plant for the expanfion of its roots, on which fo much of the Planter's future hopes depends, that he had much better give up the thoughts of raifing feedlings, and purchafe what he may want from a nurfery man, than attempt it on a ftiff clay or poor hungry gravel. This I can affert from many inftances within my own knowledge; and fo far are the beft modern practitioners in planting, from co-inciding with the long-received opinion, that a nurfery ought to be on a poorer foil, than that which is defigned for the plantation; that Kennedy is confident, every nurfery-man in England will join him in opinion, of the propriety of having trees raifed in ground equally good, at leaft if not *better*, than that on which they are to be planted: and contends, that for different purpofes, which we fhall ftate hereafter, the nurfery cannot be made too deep, nor be too well prepared.—Boutcher, who allows the fpecious

appear-

appearance of the theory, and had continued the practice for some time himself, says that he found, from repeated experiments, the bad effects of committing young and tender seedlings to poor ground; and insists on the absolute necessity of their being nursed in a generous soil, in order to promote that vigorous growth, which alone can enable them to struggle with the inconveniencies they may be subject to at a later period: from my own experience, I have known trees which had been transplanted from a poor nursery in which their bark had been hardened, to remain for years at a stand until they were cut to the ground, and had then, as I may say, received a second birth; whilst the fir from the same nursery, which could not be cut down, though they continued to grow; yet by their slender stems in proportion to their height, and a certain blackish hue, have evinced for many years the injury they sustained in the early part of their growth; in fact, the success of a tree when transplanted, depends on the goodness of its root; or in other words, on the quantity of fibres, which open as so many mouths to suck in nourishment; some of these fibres muſt be loſt in tranſplanting; and that ſoil which produces the moſt of them, promiſes the leaſt check to the tree on its removal.—The richeſt and melloweſt ſoil, is undoubtedly moſt capable of producing vegetation, and conſequently furniſhing the moſt fibres; this will appear moſt ſtrongly, if we apply to analogy, is not the beſt fed calf the moſt likely to make the largeſt bull?—Is not every animal the hardier and more capable of labour, when grown up, for having been plentifully and vigorouſly nouriſhed in its infancy; let not the Planter then be afraid of making his nurſery rich by any ſtrong manure he can compaſs; I ſhould wiſh my nurſery to be rich enough to produce cellery without dung, and deep enough for liquorice.—A miſtaken notion has prevailed, that a deep ſoil makes the roots too deep; but experience ſhews, we have nothing to apprehend from this circumſtance in young trees, and frequent tranſplantation prevents it in thoſe of an older growth.

I recommend frequent digging the ground near the plants in the nurſery; it operates on
the

the root, as clipping does on the branches of a hedge: it thickens and encreafes the fibres near the main ftem, and forms them into a compact ball for tranfplantation.—As to the depth it fhould be prepared to, that depends on the purpofes for which the plants are wanting, viz. nine inches deep for trees to be tranfplanted in the nurfery, and nearly double that depth for thofe that are to be planted out at once from the *feed bed* to where they are to remain, in order to gain that extenfion of root fo effentially neceffary for the fuccefs of the Planter on *fhallow* foils: Kennedy confiders this fo material an object, as to be furprized that the raifing of trees for this purpofe, has never been made a diftinct article in the nurfery bufinefs—hence it follows clearly, that the directions for the preparation and management of the nurfery muft depend in a great meafure on the nature and fituation of the foil to be planted, which may for the fake of order be confidered in general under the following heads:

1ft. Lay

1ſt. Lay ground or tillage land of a ſufficient depth to bear trench plowing, but in a bleak expoſure.

2dly. Natural woodland amongſt ſhrubs and thickets.

3dly. A fertile ſoil, with good ſhelter.

4thly. A dry ſhifting ſand.

5thly. A ſhallow ſtoney or moory ſoil.

6thly. A deep, dry, or heathy moor.

7thly. Actual red bog.

I ſhall ſay ſomething of the management of the nurſery for each of the above purpoſes; and after a few obſervations on the manner of pruning trees for tranſplantation, and the beſt method of conducting the buſineſs of planting in general, proceed to conſider the above heads ſeparately, and give ſuch directions as reſult from my own experience, or have been recommended

commended by the beſt practical writers on the ſubject.

For planting under the four firſt heads viz. *lay ground, in a bleak expoſure*—in *woodland*—*on a good ſoil with ſhelter, and in a dry ſhifting ſand;* the management in the nurſery may be pretty much the ſame, with this difference, that for the firſt and laſt of theſe heads, the ſhorteſt and ſtouteſt bodied plants muſt be choſen: whereas in a good ſoil well ſheltered, plants of a larger ſize, and which have remained longer in the nurſery, may be ſafely planted; and in woodlands, amongſt a thicket of hazel, thorn, &c. ſtill taller plants, and even thoſe which have remained in the nurſery, to a ſize which would render their removal in any other ſituation very precarious, may here be ventured out with the utmoſt probability of ſucceſs.

The plants for all the above purpoſes, ſhould be pricked out from the ſeed bed, upon ſmall ridges or beds about three feet broad, three rows in each bed, at a foot aſunder, which will give the nurſery-man an opportunity of under-cutting

ting the roots of the *deciduous* plants with a sharp spade, at about eight inches under the surface, the year after their first transplantation—in these beds, if they remain two years after this operation, they will form such a matt of fibres, that they may be removed with the greatest certainty of success, to any ground deep enough to receive their roots, which at the same time, will be of such a weight as to balance their heads, and keep them upright with little or no trouble; a matter of no small moment in open grounds, especially such as by tillage, or other preparation, have been brought into a state sufficiently mellow for the reception of the plants.—There cannot be a better method than the above, for all deciduous trees, except oak, Spanish-chesnut, and walnut, whose treatment I should wish to vary so far, as not to subject them to a second removal; but would sow the acorns, chesnuts or walnuts, about four inches asunder, on little square seed beds, about four feet broad; and the second year would undercut them as above, about a foot below the surface, from thence they may be removed at four years old, with nearly all their roots, will suffer

very

very little check on removal, and if they like the under ſtratum of their new ſituation, will in a very few years make as ſtrong and penetrating tap roots as if they had been ſown there, with the additional advantage of having at the ſame time vigorous lateral ones; where *timber* is the object, I ſtrongly recommend the above practice, but where the *fruit* of the Walnut or Cheſnut is in contemplation, &c. they ſhould be tranſplanted two or three times at leaſt in the Nurſery previous to their final removal.

For *a ſhallow thin ſoil*, whether *moory or rocky*, Kennedy recommends three year old plants from the *Seed-bed* out of a deep well prepared Nurſery; taken up with all their tap roots and every fibre poſſible; and as Mr. Forteſcue for planting in *red bog*, adviſes the placing the extremity of the tap root in a little cleft in the end of a ſtick, and thus inſerting it in a hole previouſly made with a crow or ſtake, preſſing the ground cloſe to the root with the foot, it is obvious that plants for ſuch purpoſes, ought to be *ſeedlings* raiſed as before in a Nurſery which has been *trenched* and well prepared to a *good depth*.

Thus

Thus for the production of plants for every foil and fituation, a fertile well prepared Nurfery will be found the beft; but with this difference, that in general it is to be made *deepeft* where the plants are intended for a *fhallow foil:* this feeming contradiction will be explained when we come to the different methods of planting in different fituations.

As to the pruning of trees at the time of tranfplanting, it is difficult to give general directions; ever-greens certainly fhould not be touched with the knife, except where a root is greatly bruifed or torn which had then better be cut off, or where a long ftubborn tap-root prevents the tree fettling well in the ground; in which cafe a nick half through with the knife, gives an opportunity of bending the tap-root horizontally, which will then throw out ftrong fhoots both from its extremity and from the fpot immediately above the incifion: I prefer this to cutting off the tap-root as is generally practifed; as to the lower branches of Fir, they fhould never be pruned off at planting; thofe clofe to

the

the ground may be of material ufe by throwing a few fhovels of earth over their extremities and pinning them to the ground in the nature of laying, which will keep the plant fteady until the tree has taken to the foil; but then the branches fhould by no means be fuffered to take root. Deciduous trees of any fize fhould be pruned in the Nurfery if poffible, a year before tranfplanting; in general a young tree fhould be encouraged in its lateral branches, and at the time of planting the great ones only fhould be fhortened, leaving the fmall ones on, which will detain the fap in the ftem and prevent the tree from being too much drawn and top-heavy; the beft form of a well pruned tree being that of a cone or nearly the natural form of a *Fir*, it thus becomes more fteady againft the winds, which do more mifchief to young plantations in Ireland, than froft, drought or any other circumftance.

The Beech is mentioned by Boulcher as an exception to the above method of pruning; and confiderable experience has confirmed me in the truth of this remark, that the lefs wood is taken off

off a Beech at the time of tranfplanting, the fooner it recovers the removal; when once well eftablifhed, it will bear the amputation of limbs, which would have caufed a canker in the ftem immediately above the wound, had it been done at the time of tranfplanting; it is an inattention to this circumftance which has given Beech the character of a difficult tree to tranfplant; however, care fhould be taken that there are not two leaders left on, and where fuch a fecond leader proceeds from the middle of the tree with a ftem nearly equal to that which you wifh to ftand, the beft way is to cut it off *clofe* if under an inch diameter; if over that fize juft above a fmall branch at fix inches or a foot from the principal ftem; this will prevent the danger of a canker, and is in general the beft way of cutting off ftrong branches if not done the year before removal, when they may, and indeed ought to be cut *clofe to the ftem.*

In recommending the foregoing rule for *pruning* in preference of that given us by Mr. Speechly who from his practice at Welbeck directs us to cut off all the branches from the ftem for
half

half way up and to fhorten the whole into a piramidical form, I differ from fo eminent a planter with great deference, but I prefer leaving more of the lower branches at the time of planting from having frequently obferved trees which were treated in any other manner to encreafe confiderably in their *heads*, whilft the *ftems* not only continued at a ftand, but became hard and hidebound and required to be flit down the bark with a knife, which the gardeners ufually term *bleeding*, before they recovered their vigour, when the tree is once eftablifhed and in a thriving ftate, the bottom branches fhould every year for fome years, have a tire or more pruned off, which will not only contribute to the beauty of the tree, but greatly improve the future timber.

Where the extremities of the roots are bruifed in removal, they fhould be taken off with a floping cut with the face downwards; in general the lefs the *root* is pruned the better, but if large bunches of matted fibres have been fuffered to dry in the air on taking up, they fhould be cut away or at leaft fhortened as otherwife

wife no new shoots will be produced from them; and from this circumstance, I venture to caution the Planter against relying too implicitly on the receipt for removing large trees given by *Evelyn* and others, however specious it appears in theory, viz: cutting the tree all round and filling the trench up, and so leaving it for one year before removal: I can say from my own experience on many beech trees so managed, that those of the same age and upon the same ground, which had been removed *at once* without such preparation in a very few years far surpassed them; the great masses of tufted fibres which were carried to the new ground in the former method growing mouldy and rotting away, and the roots which had supplied them the year before not being in condition to throw out new ones; whilst those trees of about twenty years old, which were taken at once to their new destination, produced healthy fibres which soon became vigorous roots—if a Planter wishes to try Evelyn's method, he should by all means let the tree stand *two years at least* after cutting the roots before it's removal, *at which time* he may prune off the smallest fibres

fibres of the laſt year; and carry only the more hardened and woody part of the roots to the new ſite.

Beech and ſycamore were the trees on which my experiments were made; perhaps oak, as having naturally fewer fibres, might have anſwered better in the method recommended by Mr. Evelyn.—Too much care cannot be taken to prevent the effects of drying winds and froſt on the roots of trees, at the time of taking up and tranſplanting; a tub of water thickened with earth to the conſiſtence of cream, ſhould be ready to receive *ſeedling plants* by all means, and moſt others, in general as they are taken up; and cloſe boxed carts ſhould be prepared for larger trees, in which they may be placed *perpendicularly* on the bottom of their roots; many trees are ſpoiled by carrying them horizontally, one ſide of the root is generally broken to pieces, and the cock ſhoots of the fir are injured in taking them out of the cart in that poſition; the more hands, and the abler the men employed, in taking up trees of every ſize out of a nurſery, the ſafer they will be got up.

When

When the ground is once opened, a ſtrong ſteady pull will raiſe a tree, with nearly all its roots uninjured; but if there is not ſtrength ſufficient for that purpoſe, the roots are ſhortened, and often cut to pieces with the ſpade, to facilitate the removal.—In carrying on a large plantation with effect, much depends on the method of arranging the workmen: that which is given by Mr. Speechly, in his Deſcription of the great Improvements by planting at Welbeck, appears to be made with much judgment; he divides his workmen into four claſſes, viz. *takers-up*, *pruners*, *carriers*, and *planters*.—Soon as the plants are taken up he beds them in the ground in the following manner; a trench is opened at leaſt fifteen inches deep, and the young trees laid in with their tops aſlant, covering their roots well, and half way up the ſtem with the earth that comes out of a ſecond trench, which is filled in like manner, and ſo on, till a ſufficiency are taken up for the preſent occaſion.

In a light ſoil, this trouble is but little; and by it they are ſecured both from the danger of their

their roots drying, and their suffering by frost: they are carried in a low-wheeled waggon from the heaps where they have been bedded, to the pruners; when they arrive, the planters and pruners assist to bed them there, in the same manner as before described; there is a portable shed for the pruners to work under, which is also convenient for the rest of the workmen, as a shelter in stormy weather; from the above heaps the plants are taken only, as fast as they are wanted for the pruners; whose work is performed as before mentioned, with an attention at all times to plant with as much roots as can possibly be kept on: as soon as they are pruned, they are taken to the *planters* by the *carriers*, who are generally a set of boys, or the worst of the labourers.—The planters go in pairs, one makes the holes, and the other sets and treads round the plants, which work they generally perform alternately.

Though Boutcher prefers spring for planting every sort of seedling; he allows he has had great success in planting fir of all ages early in *August*; and strongly recommends a trial of
this

this practice.—It is not indeed an eafy matter to afcertain the beſt feaſon for removing of trees, fo much depends on the nature of the foil and fituation.—In ſtormy fituations I prefer planting in fpring : but trees planted at this time will require more watering : in general, we may fay, that with few exceptions (amongſt which, I think the aſh is one, which though apparently a very backward tree, feems to be injured by removal late in fpring) all the deciduous trees may be planted in any month between October and their time of ſhooting into leaf; and Millar, in his early editions, mentions the beginning of May, as the beſt time to plant oak.—Boutcher and Lord Kaims agree with him ; and I have followed that practice for feveral years with fuch great fuccefs, that I venture highly to recommend it.

Out of fome thoufand oak, tranfplanted the fecond week in May, from a feedling-bed at Mr. Edgar's nurfery near the Foundling Hofpital, where they had ſtood in that rich foil 'till above four feet high fcarcely one failed though carried thirty miles to a high fituation in the
county

county of Wicklow; they were tranſplanted in the year 1778, and are now, in 1792, above twenty feet high, and thick in proportion.

Larch is another exception to autumn planting; the moſt experienced writers, recommend planting them juſt as they puſh out in ſpring. — Ever-greens in general may be planted from the beginning of April to June, and ſome kinds, as the holly, ſtill later; I have planted them with ſucceſs at Midſummer.

There is ſome reaſon however to think, that laurel and Scots-fir are exceptions, the latter of which, from repeated experiments, I would not wiſh to plant after the month of March, whilſt the former may be ſafely planted in November; or even the beginning of December, when the weather is ſoft.—Perhaps on the whole, we ſhall find, that the beſt general rule we can eſtabliſh for removing *evergreens*, is to tranſplant either *early* in autumn, or when their buds begin to ſhoot in ſpring.

In every young plantation, if there is not a natuarl growth of thorn, hazel, &c. several lines of broom should be sown for shelter, the cost is little, and the effect in preserving the plants from the wind is very great.—Most deciduous trees are apt to lose the sappiness of their bark on transplantation; and I have found it of great use when I did not cut them down the second year, to draw a line as before mentioned, with a sharp knife through the bark from top to bottom, so as to let the tree spread, and prevent its being *hide-bound*.

I shall now proceed to give particular directions for planting, suited to the various soils and situations, as before specified, and first,

For lay-ground or tillage-land of a sufficient depth, to bear trench-plowing, but in a bleak exposure.

The experienced author of Hints on Planting, gives the best directions for the preparation of such ground by trench-plowing; which is to be done by a second plough following in the furrow made by the first, going as deep as possible, poffible, and with a higher mold-board, throwing the earth over the firft turned foil.

If the ground has been ploughed out of *the lay*, it muft continue in the above fituation for fome months; by which time the turf at bottom will be rotten : it fhould then be crofsploughed, and the deeper and finer the tilth is made, fo much the better, for every fucceffive operation.

In good land thus prepared, almoft any mode of planting may be adopted with fuccefs; but as fuch preparation generally implies a fmooth open furface, and confequently little fhelter ; ftrong plants about five years old, and which have been tranfplanted two years before in the nurfery, are beft fuited to the purpofe — Their height will be fuch as to efcape injury from thofe ftrong weeds which fuch a foil and preparation muft naturally produce, and the fize and weight of the roots will keep them fteady and upright, without ftaking or banking, which is a material circumftance in a plantation of any extent.

If trees of the above description cannot be easily procured, the taller evergreens may be assisted, by covering a few of their lower branches with earth in the manner of *laying*, as before mentioned, and the deciduous trees, (beech and walnut excepted) should be cut close to the ground, with a smooth sloping cut; this advice of Mr. Fortescue's he supports from his own experience, and asserts, that the first year's shoots have frequently exceeded four feet.

Mr. Fortescue's practice however, was in general, on ground pretty much covered with hazel and thorn, but where we are entirely destitute of shelter I would advise a mode recommended above one hundred and twenty years ago, by Smith, in his *England's Improvement*, in which he advises the laying of all deciduous trees sloping on the turf or sod, turned over as usually done in marking out our quickset fences, covering them with the next spade of soil; and sloping the bank which is laid over them down to the next row of plants, in order 'to conduct the rain to the roots; the rows should stand so as to give the young plants the most effectual shelter, and the

heads

heads of the sets should be cut off at the time of planting, as we do our thorn quicks, from whose free growth when thus managed, we may safely adopt the practice, where the nature of the trees and exposure of the situation would render them liable to be shaken in the ordinary mode of planting.

In less exposed situations, I should wish to defer cutting them down till after one or two years growth, when there cannot be the least doubt that the trees so managed, will in a very short time far excel those left standing.— For this purpose, the Planter should often visit his plantation, and when he sees a tree dead at top or hide-bound, he shoud cut it down within six inches at most of the ground; and where many shoots spring from the same root, all should be cut off but the strongest, and the dead wood of the old stock cut close to the young shoot.

If the land *be a stiff clay*, it may be much Improved by sand or lime, and when thus prepared there cannot be a better soil for *orchards*.— The finest in Worcester-shire and Hereford-shire

are

are on such soils; the former of these counties has long been famous for its cyder, particularly that called *Styre*, from an apple of that name, which grows better in the forest of Deane and its vicinity, than many other parts of England.

This apple is said to have been originally brought from Styria near the Tyrol, and is supposed to produce the highest flavoured cyder, when planted on a soil which contains a mixture of Iron Ore, as it generally does in the forest of Deane. We have large tracts of such soil in Ireland, on part of which it might be worth while to make the experiment; but we can never hope for a good orchard from the practice too commonly adopted, of planting large grafted apple trees on a bleak exposure.—We should plant in the first instance, as Mr. Fortescue with great judgment advises, four or five years old crab quicks or wildings (the former however are much the best,) in those spots where they are to remain as the principal fruit trees of the future orchard.—They should then be cut down and grafted or inoculated in a few years, on the young healthy shoots from the best sorts of fruit
trees.

trees. When the real crab thus grafted comes into bearing, it may be expected to continue in perfection for more than a *century*, in the mean time an immediate fupply of fruit may be obtained, if the orchard be well fheltered, by planting in the intervals dwarf apple trees, on Harlem ftocks or pitchards, which are truncheons made of the bearing boughs of fuch fort of apple trees chiefly, as throw out round the lower parts of their branches, a fort of burr or excrefcence, very much refembling the burrs of a deers horn, where it joins the head, on which part of the branch a ftrong fibrous root is fpeedily formed.

The celebrated Irifh cyder apple, called the *Cacagee*, grows very well when planted in this manner, as do feveral of the beft cyder fruits on the banks of the Black Water in the county of Waterford; but it fhould be remembered, that trees thus raifed, as well as thofe grafted on *dwarf ftocks*, though they come into bearing very foon, are of very fhort duration, we fhould not only take care to have a fucceffion, but we fhould perpetuate the beft fruits, by grafting them from time to time on the crab ftocks in the orchard, a fufficiency of which fhould be ready trained up to fingle ftems for that purpofe.

We have many places in Ireland, which, though not fuited to the apple, would anfwer the pery pears to the utmoft of our wifhes; but in this cafe, we fhould be attentive to the kinds we plant.—Thofe called in Hereford-fhire, *Taunton Squafh* and *Befbury*, are the pears moft approved of for making pery, which I have known to be fold in the neighbourhood of Rofs, in Hereford-fhire, for ten guineas the hogfhead by the maker, and that to the amount of fifty hogfheads, all the property of one perfon.

It was with this fparkling beverage that the amiable Kerles of Rofs, in Herefordfhire, better known as immortalized by Mr. Pope, under the name of the *Man of Rofs*, ufed to treat twelve of his neighbours at dinner every Thurfday,

day, felected indifcriminately from the gentlemen and farmers who attended the market of that town.—The general communication on fubjects of agriculture, &c. which naturally refulted from fuch a meeting was of advantage to both parties, whilft he afforded in himfelf an example of every focial virtue.—Though liberal to magnificence in the execution of feveral public works, for the advantage and ornament of the town, many of which ftill remain, he was fo plain in his manners, and frugal in his expences on *himfelf*, that he was enabled to extend his charity to a degree which has fince become proverbial, and to give this conftant weekly entertainment to all his neighbours in their turn; at which time his table was covered with all the beft productions of Herefordfhire, and the neighbouring counties; but no foreign wine or fpirits were ever allowed to appear, their place being amply fupplied by fine beers, Redftreak and Styre cyder, and particularly by Pery of a quality little inferior to the beft champaigne.—Some of this kind I tafted in his own parlour at Rofs, when on a tour I made a few years fince, through the cyder counties, on purpofe to gain information on the fubject of orchards.—His houfe was then converted to a well kept inn, from the mafter of which, a very well informed man, and the curate of the parifh, who dwelt with rapture on the memory of Mr. Kerles, I obtained the above particulars, as well as fome ufeful hints on cyder and pery.

The pleafure and advantages arifing from plantations of other fpecies of fruit trees befide the apple, feem to have been much better underftood in the laft century than in the prefent; many of the writers on Rural Œconomicks of thofe days, dwell with fuch heartfelt fatisfaction on the directions they give for laying out and planting their " *Labyrinths of* " *Sweets*," and " *Paradifes of Content*."—That notwithftanding the formality of ther arrangement, even a faftidious Modern Improver might be tempted to take a morning walk in them, in order to enjoy " the verdant carpets" they defcribe, " bordered with the primrofe and
" the

" the violet, and all the pride of fpring, be-
" tween the woodbine hedge, and fragrant eg-
" lantine, fheltered by the filbert, plum, quince
" and medlar, or fhaded over by the lofty wal-
" nut, chefnut, or cherry tree.

" *On whofe fprays,*
" *The Throftle chaunts his roundelays.*"

This decorated walk which is recommended to the good *hufbandman*, in many authors of the laft age, and differs very little from the modern fhrubbery, except in being formed of ftraight lines, and invariably bordered with trees which were planted for *ufe*, as well as *ornament*, was generally carried round a confiderable piece of ground, which contained the orchard properly fo called, the garden for efculent plants, and ufually feveral ponds for fifh and water-fowl.

And perhaps on the whole, a few acres could not be more agreeably or advantageoufly difpofed of, efpecially as fuch an improvement is within the compafs of many who could not afford the extent of ground, and other expences attending the practice of modern ornamental gardening.

The

The great longevity and stately growth of the walnut, chesnut, and wilding cherry, entitle them to the first rank amongst timber trees; but in order to improve their fruit, they should certainly be grafted or inoculated: this appears to be the constant practice abroad, and I have reason to think, that the difficulty we find in the process here, arises from the gardeners making use of loom or clay, in place of a strong *grafting wax*, which I have observed has been applied to all the grafted nuts which are brought from Holland.

In planting forest trees, the oak, wallnut, Spanish chesnut, elm and ash, should be our principal consideration, which may be planted at about twenty feet asunder, avoiding straight lines, for many reasons; the plantation should then be thickened up with any other sort of trees; placing Scots fir and beech in the most exposed situations, except in the neighbourhood of the sea, where the sycamore is observed to stand its effects better than either of the above.

Hazel

Hazel nuts, and the feeds of Liburnam, Portugal, Spanish, and common broom may then be scattered through them; and juniper, holly, and laurel planted towards the front, and near the opens and walks, which will be at once very ornamental; and afford good cover for game.

For planting *in natural woodland, amongst shrubs and thickets.*

It has before been observed that the tallest and weakest bodied plants may be selected for that purpose. In the spaces which they may fill amongst the shrubs and under-wood, they will certainly succeed, and make good trees, if taken up with roots proportioned to their size, and planted with care.—Experience has proved, that where hazel and white-thorn grow with vigour, almost every species of forest tree may be planted to advantage: it will only be found necessary to prevent the branches of the shrubs from over-topping, or interfering with the young shoots of the plantation, and paying a proper attention to keep the plants from being top-heavy;

heavy, as they are more apt to be in this situation than in any other, and generally exhibit such marks of luxuriant health, as appear extraordinary to those who consider the neighbouring shrubs as likely to draw all the nourishment from the *forest-trees*; but as Fortescue justly observes, Providence has wisely scattered the food of each plant over the surface of the earth, so that many trees of *different species*, will grow well in an acre of ground, where the same number of *one kind* would actually starve for want of nourishment; and we have only to view a grove of the last age, consisting of one species of trees, to be convinced of the inferiority of each tree which composes it, to one of the same age growing amongst plants of different species, though equally close and numerous.

The holes should be made amongst the shrubs, from eight to twenty feet asunder, as an open offers.—In this unwrought soil they should be considerably larger than the roots designed to be planted in them, in order to give room to the young fibres, and if made

some

fome time before the planting, fo much the better.—But the good foil, after being chopped and broken fine, fhould be returned *into the holes*: for if left on the edge till the planting feafon, as is ufually done, the *finer parts* will be wafhed by the rains into the ground, or loft amongft the grafs and leaves, fo as very much to retard the progrefs of the Planter.

For making holes in *wood-land*, a long bladed hoe, with a narrow axe on the other point, will be found to be a very ufeful inftrument, as here the roots of hazel and thorn are continually croffing the fpots where the holes fhould be made.

What we thin out of our plantations of fix or feven years growth, tho' much drawn up, may be planted in this ground with great fuccefs.— They will here recover ftrength and a proper form.—I have known larch, which had been apparently dead for fome time, of a dufky lead colour, and broke off by the cattle at three feet from the ground, where they were about an inch and a half diameter; on being removed into a hazel coppice about twelve years ago, not only to recover their natural colour, and make new leaders, but become moſt beautiful trees, and are at this time, above thirty feet high.

When we have not the advantage of *natural wood-land*, but poſſeſs a *good ſoil* and *ſtrong land ſhelter*, well furniſhed plants either from a nurſery, or the thinning of plantations, about five or ſix feet high, may be removed with ſucceſs, and even thoſe of a larger ſize, if ſufficient care is taken to raiſe them with as much roots as poſſible, and carry them without injury to their new deſtination.

For this laſt purpoſe, there cannot be a better machine than that firſt introduced into this kingdom by Mr. Robinſon, a Scottiſh Engineer.

It conſiſts of a pole about ſixteen or eighteen feet long, divided at the ſtronger end into two branches, which are morticed into an axle-tree, over which a piece of timber is bolted, about a foot high, with a hollow on the upper

per part fix inches wide and four deep, which
ſhould be dreſſed very round and ſmooth; to
this axle-tree, which muſt be ſeven feet long,
a pair of high and very ſtrong cart-wheels
are occaſionally fitted.——The hollowed piece
of timber, being firſt well covered with
ſtraw or a mat, is then applied cloſe to the
trunk of the tree; and the pole, which will
in this ſituation lie up the ſtem, is to be
tied cloſe as poſſible along it, putting ſtraw
between the bark and the cords; the roots
having been previouſly cut round, about three
feet from the trunk on every ſide, to the depth
of the under fibres, and a rope applied to the
top of the pole; the latter is drawn downwards,
and with it the ſtem of the tree, which conſequently forces up the *whole root* from its under bed with all its fibres, and leaves it hang-
ing on the axle-tree between the wheels; it
is then drawn with the root foremoſt over the
hole deſigned for its reception, and the pole being freed from the ſtem, the latter regains its
natural poſition, and the earth being carefully
laid about, and inſerted with a blunt pointed
ſtick, amongſt the roots, and the whole well
watered,

watered, the tree will scarcely exhibit the least mark of removal in the second year.

It is evident that this machine not only accelerates the taking up of large trees, but carries all their roots without injury; which is seldom the case when they are obliged to be brought any distance in any other manner of conveyance; and as this machine will also be found of the utmost service in rooting up such trees as a Planter may wish to remove, without an intention of planting again; but where the roots would prove injurious or disagreeable if suffered to remain in the ground.—I annex three explanatory drawings, and will venture to assert, that with a little attention to *Boutcher's* advice of twice transplanting, and digging round the roots in the nursery, trees may be thus removed of such a size, as will afford, not only immediate decoration, but considerable shelter; it must however, be always remembered, that a great extent of plantation can never be effected with the waste of time and expence of labour, which such heavy operations require.—They are only suited to the gratification of a Planters wishes in particular instances—from such you can indulge but slender expectations of future fame, as an improver of your country—a few dotting trees will never change the face of an extensive tract of naked ground: in such situations,

> " *Rich the robe,*
> " *And ample let it flow, that Nature wears*
> " *On her thron'd eminence: where'er she takes*
> " *Her horizontal march, pursue her step*
> " *With sweeping train of forest; hill to hill,*
> " *Unite with prodigality of shade.*"

Mason's English Garden.

Plate I. *Figure 1.*

Shews the pole divided at the end, and inserted into the axle tree, with the hollow'd piece of timber over it.

Figure 2.

Represents the machine brought close over the root of the tree, and the pole tied up along the stem.

Figure 3.

Shews the manner in which the root will fit between the wheels; when the pole has been drawn down, the little wheel behind may be used by inserting its frame into the pole, as the single wheel of a plough usually is done; but except for very large trees, and such as are to be carried a considerable distance, there is no occasion for this third wheel.

For the fourth divifion of foils: viz. *a dry fhifting fand*: the plants fhould be no higher than barely to efcape being covered with the drifts.—On fuch land, ftrong weeds do not abound, and the fooner the plant is enured to the foil after the feedling fibres attain a reafonable firmnefs, the better chance of its fucceeding: we cannot affift its growth by ftirring the ground in this drifting fand; for as the fault of the foil is want of cohefion, it is not advifeable to dig amongft the trees when once planted. The holes fhould be made at the time of planting, and if the expence would not be very great, a cart of mold fhould attend the operation, and another with water; and when the holes are half filled up over the roots, fome water fhould be poured on, and the remainder of the earth and fand thrown in.

Though fuch a driving fand feems the leaft likely of any to gratify the Planter's wifhes, we have feveral inftances of its producing a great growth of timber.—Mr. Speechly defcribes thofe very fuccefsful plantations of the Duke of Portland at Welbeck, to have been

made

made on such a soil, which he says is called in Nottingham-shire, *Forest-lands*, being a continuation of hills and dales, covered merely with a mixture of sand and gravel, the hills abounding mostly with the latter, and the vallies with the former; as the smaller particles are by the wind and rains brought from time to time from the high grounds to the lower.

In a well sheltered part of such a valley, the nursery is formed, which is to supply plants for a considerable tract of the surrounding hills.— The plants raised there for that purpose are oak, beech, larch, Spanish chesnut, Weymouth pine, and all sorts of fir, (the Scots excepted,) together with some inferior sorts for the purpose of shelter, amongst which, the birch is most prized.

The quantities raised on these sandy valleys at the Duke of Portland's must be very great indeed, for the supply of such extensive tracts of plantation, from sixty to a hundred acres being often planted, as Mr. Speechly states, in one season, and that considered only

as

as a part of one defign for clothing the great chain of hills above defcribed.

The land intended to be planted, is well ploughed and manured with lime, about twenty-four barrels to the acre, for a crop of turnips: when the turnips are eaten off, the ground is ploughed with a trenching plough, to the depth of twelve inches.—This deep ploughing is of the utmoft fervice both to the future growth of the plants, and to the eafe of carrying on the operation of planting.

The manner of difpofing the trees in the plantations at Welbeck, depends much on the particular fhape of the part to be planted; and on the tafte of the perfon employed at the time.

Between the hills towards the outfide of the plantation, ridings are frequently left from fixty to a hundred yards in breadth; which are contracted towards the middle of the woods to ten or twelve yards: on the tops of the hills, where
there

there are plains, lawns are left of an acre or two in extent, which form a pleasing variety; in some of them cedars of Lebanon are planted at irregular distances to form hereafter an open grove.—This tree seems peculiarly adapted to this light moist land; on the outsides of the plantation next the ridings, evergreens are scattered profusely, hollies, laurels, yews, junipers, &c.—Sometimes each sort by itself, and at other times intermixed, but, always so as to avoid the appearance of a regular edging, now and then a rare foreign tree is introduced, such as the Virginian julip tree, &c. &c.

When the ground is laid out into quarters for planting, certain parts are assigned to beech, larch, Spanish chesnut, &c. which are introduced in irregular patches, through the plantations, with an excellent effect, from the diversity of shades, especially in those parts of the forest, where four or five large hilly points meet in the same valley, and tend, as it were to one center,

In carrying on the work of planting, the largeſt trees of every ſort are got in firſt; were they to proceed otherwiſe, the making a hole for a large rooted tree, after the ſmall ones were planted as thick as they ought to be, would cauſe great confuſion.—Birch is generally the tree to begin with, as it bears removal perfectly well. At the height of ſix or ſeven feet, of thoſe, or rather of a leſs ſize, three or four hundred are planted on one acre; and nearly the ſame number of their firſt ſized oak; then the maſſes of larch, birch, and Spaniſh cheſnut are got in; and ſome of a ſmaller ſize of the ſame ſpecies are inſerted through the whole: then a number of ſmaller ſized oak, and laſtly, theſe are thickened with ſmall ſeedling birch, the whole made up to about two thouſand plants of different ſizes and ages to the Engliſh acre, great care being taken, that they are as free from ſtraight lines and regularity as poſſible, both to give a natural air to the plantation, and to avoid the effect of penetrating winds.

When the planting is finiſhed, a conſiderable quantity of acorns, keys, and maſt, are inſerted in short drills of two or three feet in length amongst the young trees, which in some situations may be considered as the most certain source of a good growth of timber.—This leads to the progress of their oak at Welbeck, of which Mr. Speechly gives two instances, one of twenty-eight, the other of fifty years growth; in the former they are about twenty-six feet high, and about eighteen inches round: in the latter they exceed sixty feet, and are somewhat more than three in circumference; but are very long and fair in the bole, without knots or lateral shoots, from their having been at first thickly planted, and regularly thinned only as they required room.

In addition to this satisfactory account from Mr. Speechly, we have the experience of the late Duke of Cumberland on Bagshot, as an encouragement to the owners of sandy gravely wastes—here a loose red sand, or hard whitish gravel and spar, seemingly a decomposition of manganese and granite, mixed with a small portion of black turfy mould formed the whole

of

of the foil of that great tract, which he speedily covered, not only with fir of various kinds, but with Spanish chesnut, laurel, lignum vitæ, juniper and other ever-greens and shrubs.

The next division, viz. *the shallow rocky foil*, is peculiarly adapted to improvement by plantation, which will be found to be not only the most pleasing, but the most œconomic measure we can adopt.

For the better carrying the Planter's design into execution here, I shall follow *Kennedy*, who seems to have had great experience on such foils.

As it will be necessary to plant in every spot where a little earth can be got amongst the rocks, he recommends the use of light long bladed hoes, with a pick on the other end: with the broad end, or a sharp narrow spade, the turf should be pared off as thin as possible; with the narrow end, the ground must be picked up about six inches deep; taking out such stones as the hoe loosens, for the space of about two feet diameter,

ter, and avoiding the rocks; when they intervene, so as to prevent a hole being made for a greater space than six feet, three or four holes may be made very near together in the next interval, as the trees, though close on one side, will have sufficient air on the other, and in such situations, the Planter must avail himself of every possible spot which will admit a tree.

The earth thus stirred up in the hole, may be left in it, and the turf which was first pared off, turned upside down, and laid on one side until it has been well moistened by autumnal rains; immediately after which, the trees should be planted. Spring would be a bad season for this work, from the danger of drought, which would be doubly destructive in this dry, burning soil, and for the same reason, the turf pared off ought not to be put in the *bottom* of the hole, as is usually done in other situations, as it is here generally light and spungy, and full of sedge, which would admit the parching winds, and prevent the plants taking root.

Having

Having thus waited 'till after the firſt heavy autumnal rains, take up as many *ſeedlings* from a deep well prepared nurſery as can be planted in one day, preſerve all the roots poſſible, and let them be carried to your plantation in a flat baſket covered with wet moſs.— A ſpace of about ten inches broad muſt be opened in the center of each hole, which may be done by a chop of a broad ſpade, and turning it once about; in this the ſeedling plant muſt be laid *horizontally*, with all its roots ſpread out about three or four inches deep if you can; then raiſe up the head of the plant juſt at the junction of the root with the ſtem, and put the earth cloſe up to it; prick the reſt of the hole lightly with a ſpade, and cover it with the turf, graſs ſide down, after firſt making a cut in one ſide to introduce the ſtem of the plant, which will be more effectually kept in an upright poſture by this, than by looſe earth, and is preſerved by it at the ſame time from the effect of drying winds.

This is certainly an excellent mode of planting in a ſhallow ſoil, but I have ſome doubts whether

whether it might not be better at the time of planting to cut down the deciduous trees (Birch and Walnut excepted) at about two inches from the furface; in this cafe the new fhoot will be perpendicular, and never have the leaft inclination to another pofition, which is not the cafe in Kennedy's mode, as he candidly admits, by directing the top of the tree to be turned to the North, that the fun's influence may tend to keep the ftem in an upright pofition.

In planting as above, as well as in every other fituation, though the holes are *prepared*, two men fhould always be together at putting in the plants; one fhould be on his knees, holding the plant and fpreading its roots, whilft the other with a fpade or fhovel, throws on the mould in fuch a manner, that the fine particles are equally diftributed amongft the fibres.—The roots of no trees fhould be expofed to the air if poffible, but thofe of *feedlings* in particular, the nature of their fibres render them peculiarly fufceptible of injury, and a want of attention in this point, has often
rendered

rendered ineffectual all the preparation of the ground, and other care in planting.

In spring, acorns, maft or other tree feeds may be fown in the holes where the plants have failed, chopping the turned fod through the earth in the hole, or placing it at bottom if not fufficiently mellow; and as there is little danger to be apprehended from weeds in this ground, a fine growth may be expected from feed, infomuch that if you do not abound in feedling plants, you may leave in *autumn* every fecond or third hole unplanted, for the purpofe of receiving the feeds in *fpring*.

For planting *in a fhallow moor, without rock, of a uniform furface, and a foft and wet foil.*— We have an excellent guide in the author of the Treatife on the *Pinus Silveftris.*—His practice feems indeed to have been confined to fuch a foil.

I fhall therefore, tranfcribe thofe parts of his work which I think moft inftructive for cultivating this useful tree, which, as Fortescue observes, is never out of place, and flourishes in every soil and every climate from the sandy plains of Hesse Darmstadt, to the craggy mountains of North Britain; which may be planted in our wet bogs, and will, at the same time, form the most beautiful covering for our dryest and bleakest hills.

He objects to tranfplanting this fpecies of fir in a nurfery, and putting them out at three or four years old, both from the hazard they will run in removal at that age, and from the great inconvenience, when feveral hundreds of acres are to be planted in one feafon, which is frequently the cafe at prefent in Scotland.

He advifes that the plants may be removed at two years old, from the feed bed to the place defigned for their future growth; if it be a bare heath or fhallow moor, not productive of coarfe grafs or ftrong weeds, they will foon get above the heath, if only their tops appear when planted.—On fuch ground, no holes need be made, a long narrow fpade, with a ftrong foot-hold on one fide, is forced as deep into the ground as the foot can prefs it, and as it is drawn gently out, a little plant is flipped into the opening before or behind the fpade as moft convenient, by a boy who carries the plants in a little bafket, with wet mofs on them; but if the weather is dry or windy, it is the better way to have the plants brought into the field in a veffel of water, in which earth has been mixed to the confiftence of pap, from which fmall parcels of feedlings may be taken out as they are wanted.

After the plant is inferted in the cleft made by the fpade, the ground is preffed clofe about it with the foot, and nothing further is neceffary to the work, which may be performed at the rate of one fhilling per thoufand; a man with his two little attendants planting two thoufand in one day with great eafe.

As the author computes the number to an Englifh acre, it would take juft feven thoufand eight hundred and forty to an Irifh acre, to have the trees at three feet every way from each other.—This I allow to be a great number, more than twice what I have ever known to be planted: but the Author afferts, if nothing but Scots fir is intended in the plantation, they fhould not be at a greater diftance,
not

not only for the purpofe of affording each other fhelter on bleak expofures, but as it is the excellency of the fir for timber to grow ftraight and tall as poffible, free from knots, and nearly of equal thicknefs from top to bottom, to all which, thick planting certainly contributes: in this, he ftates we are directed by Nature in the growth of the wild fir, which frequently ftands much clofer together than is here required; yet when old, they produce mafts of prodigious length, of the fineft grain, and free from knots: Their clofenefs and ftruggle to get their tops to the air, conducing to their height and even growth, whilft their near approach caufes their fuperfluous fide branches to die, and the rubbing of one tree againft another, as agitated by the wind, divefts them of the little rotten ftumps; the place where they grew is foon covered over with a firm wood, and the ftem becomes fmooth, encreafing by fuperadded growths without the mark of a branch having ever been on it.

The

That the beſt foreign timber has thus been produced, appears from comparing its grain with what we raiſe in a different way; the latter being ſuffered to grow in an open ſpace, without any thing to interrupt the ſide ſhoots, ſoon becomes a broad headed buſh: the ſide branches being often as ſtrong as the middle ſhoot, and the bottom of the ſtem conſiderably groſſer than the upper part, and through the whole a mere conjunction of knots.—The former on the other hand nearly of an equal ſize throughout, free from knots, and of ſo fine a grain or reed, as the workmen call it, (which is in fact, no more than the annual encreaſe of growth) that it is ſcarcely to be diſtinguiſhed by the naked eye: but has by the help of a glaſs, been counted to the ſurprizing number of four hundred Lamina in the ſpace of one foot, plainly indicating that the tree muſt have taken at leaſt two hundred years to come to that ſize.

The cloſeneſs of their early growth he alſo aſſerts has a tendency to produce more heart or red wood in a given time, which is the criterion

of

of the merit of this timber, at the time of felling.

What an encouragement is here held out to the cloathing of our nearly barren mountains with this useful tree, when the slowness of its growth in the diameter of its stem, tends to its perfection; and where the necessary closeness in the beginning would afford such thinnings, as in many parts of Ireland would produce a most profitable and speedy return.

Spruce fir may be planted at once from the seedling-bed, in the manner directed for the Scots, except that they need not be planted so close, and should not be removed until *three years* old; but as this tree bears removal very well at any size under four feet, and is not of such general use, nor so well suited to the soil of Ireland in general as the former, I think it had better be once transplanted in the nursery.—Silver fir, is of so slow a growth for the first three years, that it can never be propagated but by transplantation; when it is two

or

or three feet high it removes with great fuccefs, and on a ſtiff ſtubborn foil, where other evergreens fcarcely make any progrefs, I have known this beautiful tree grow to great perfection; it will bear the fea air, and a very bleak expofure; but it amply repays the advantages of a milder fituation: two of thofe in a valley in a deep fandy foil at Mount-Ufher, in the county of Wicklow, meafuring twelve feet round at fix feet from the ground, and were above a hundred feet high many years ago.

Fortefcue afferts the advantage of planting Weymouth pine in *Woodlands*, at once from the *feed bed*; and from my own experience, I can vouch the fuccefs of this practice: of one hundred planted in the county of Wicklow, from the feed bed, about twenty years ago, ninety-eight remain, many of them above forty feet high, and meafuring from thirty inches to four feet four inches in circumference; they were three years old when tranfplanted.

It

It is not, however, eafy to afcertain the foil in which the different fpecies of fir make the greateft progrefs; thofe difpofed to run down-wards like the Scots, filver fir, and pinafter, will grow on the tops of dry banks, or narrow double ditches; but I have never known a fpruce fir, or Weymouth pine to thrive in fuch fituations.—Shelter, and I believe a mellow foil are requifite to bring the latter to perfection: thofe I have before mentioned grow in fuch a foil, with a fubftratum of loofe red earth to a great depth.

I fhould have faid the fame of the fpruce fir, (as feveral I have on that kind of ground, have made a moft rapid progrefs, many of them being more than four feet fix inches in girth, at twenty-five years from the feed) had I not feen remarkable fine trees of this fpecies in very different foils, thofe, for example, at Glofter in the King's county have grown to the greateft perfection, in a black peaty moor, over a ftiff gravelly clay remarkably fteril: Thofe at Ballykillcavan, in the Queen's county, were moft beautiful,

beautiful, before an improving gardener cut off all their weeping branches; they feem to grow on a dry limeftone gravel, and Boutcher fpeaks highly of the merit of the fpruce, as fuited to hungry deep *till* and *clays*, where he afferts they would in a fhort time change the cold and gloomy appearance of fuch inhofpitable tracts of land: but whatever may be the foil, its roots feem to demand room to fpread on the furface, nor fhould thofe trees be fuffered to continue clofe together for any length of time; they have a natural inclination to grow ftraight and upright, and do not require to ftand fo thick for the purpofe of improving their timber, as is recommended for the Scots fir: When they have not been judicioufly thinned, I have known whole groves of fourteen years growth fuddenly decay, to the great difappointment of the planter, and difcredit of this beautiful tree, which by proper attention might have been preferved in full vigour. It is an indifputable fact, that the timber when of a proper age, and fuffered to ftand 'till the knots have been covered for the fpace of eighteen or twenty feet, is excellent

cellent for every purpofe to which white or yellow deal is applicable; and every planter muft allow, that in whatever foil it agrees with, no tree can produce a fpeedier or more effectual fhelter, whilft at the fame time by its lively verdure, clofe foliage, and picturefque difpofition of its weeping branches, (circumftances always to be obferved when the tree is in a perfect thriving ftate) it is peculiarly adapted to feveral purpofes of rural decoration.

AVONDALE WOODHOUSE
Designed &c. by S. H.

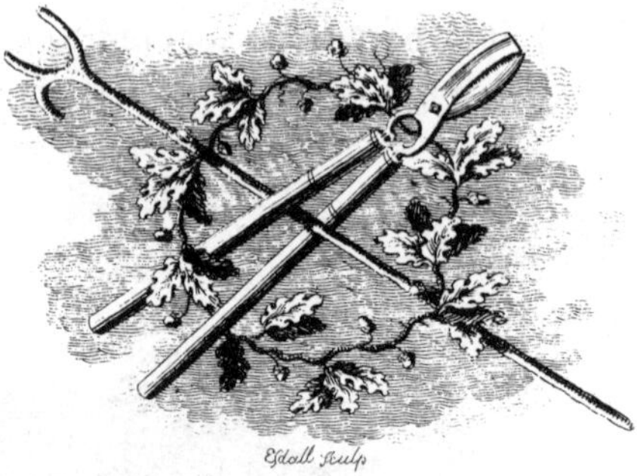
Esdall Sculp

ON

PRUNING,

AND THE MANAGEMENT OF

WOODS.

HAVING now gone through the tafk I originally propofed, of comparing the works of the moft approved Authors on the fubject of planting, with the refult of my own experience, and adapting as much as lay in my power the variety of directions they contain, to the foils and fituations for which they appear to have been refpectively intended; I fhall offer a few obfervations on the management of plantations of *fome years* ftanding, when the care and attention which has been beftowed on them at the time of planting, fhall have produced that *luxuriant growth*, which, whilft it gratifies the planter's wifhes at the moment, would utterly

defeat

defeat them in the end, if not skilfully directed and kept within proper bounds.—I shall not however greatly enlarge upon the subject of *pruning*, as exclusive of my wish to give this little treatise the merit of being *concise* at least, if it shall lay claim to nothing more, I have not found those contradictions in Authors with respect to that branch of the planter's art, which are to be observed in most others; it being universally admitted, that the heavy use of the knife or saw on the side branches, though prevented from being injurious by the admission of frost or rain, as certainly may be done by the skill of the workman and application of Mr. Forefayth's and other compositions, still tends to weaken the *stem*, and encrease the head so as to make the tree *top-heavy;* and thus either loosens the root or produces in the future timber what the English woodmen call windshakes, whilst on the other hand the neglect of cutting off in time the ill placed luxuriant branches, permits improper boughs to take the lead, and fills the timber with unsightly knots ; the want of timely thinning has the same effect on a plantation,

which

which too severe pruning of the stem produces, the plants in both cases being drawn up to weak slender poles. On the whole, no better general rule can be given than that, of never suffering any part of a tree to interfere with its neighbour for a *second season*. By this rule judiciously applied, you may continually extend your plantations, whilst they are composed of trees *young* enough to bear *transplanting*. At a more advanced age, the saw and long-handled pruning sheers will be found to be very useful instruments; but if after this, they still stand too close together, the *axe* must do its office, taking care at the same time, that the falling of one tree does not injure another, which is best prevented by a careful labourer attending on the *feller*, with a long pole, whose top is furnished with an iron fork and a hook on one side of it, by which he either draws the falling tree towards him, or pushes it off, so as best to keep clear of the branches or stem of those trees which are designed *to remain*. A considerable profit may thus be made of our plantations or coppice woods, even of a very few years growth, and

both

both may in time be converted into open groves, where the branching heads of well grown healthy timber trees, at thirty feet afunder, fhall afford more fhade and fhelter, than ten times their number fuffered to crowd each other, in the ordinary method of management; the *over-ftands* here injuring the underwood, only as the former gradually arrives at perfection; thus warm and fheltered by their clofenefs when young, and thinned from time to time as they want room, they never become *hide-bound* or *rampiked*, but will at the fecond fall of the coppice-wood, be worth three times at leaft, the purchafe of the fee-fimple of the ground they occupy, after repaying the fum they might have fold for at the time of referving them with intereft, and alfo the lofs the underwood may have fuftained by their overfhading it; as it fhould always be taken into confideration, that the value of an oak under twenty-five years growth, bears no fort of proportion to that of one of fifty: A fine faplin of the former age, not being worth more at this day than half a crown at moft, (the bark included,) whilft I have known oaks

of

of the latter to fell from twenty to thirty shillings each, and in some instances as I shall state hereafter for nearly double that sum.*

---

* From my own experience, and the best information I can procure on the subject, the following is a fair estimate of the value of oak of different ages in the county of *Wicklow*, and I believe it will not be found to vary much in other parts of the kingdom.

An acre of coppice wood from twenty to twenty-five years growth, in which there are no reserves from a past fall, may be worth *thirty pounds*.

It will require twenty-four such trees as usually compose a coppice of that age, and which has not been regularly thin'd, to produce on an average, a barrel of bark of twelve stone, worth in summer 1793, *fifteen shillings*, which was then considered very dear. The poles of such a coppice sell from *four* to *seven shillings* per dozen.

One tree of fifty years growth, will produce a barrel of bark. The timber of such a tree is worth from *twelve* to *twenty shillings*.—A tree of seventy-five years growth may be worth from *four* to *seven pounds*, according to its form, and the demand for the particular timber it contains; the more *crooked* in general the more valuable.

From hence we may fairly make the following calculation, *viz.* that an acre of coppice wood of twenty-five

THIS great difproportion in the value of trees of different ages, throws a ftrong light on that part of my fubject, in which I confefs I am on every account,

---

five years growth, in which eighty of the beft young oak are now marked as referves, and the remainder felled this year, will in twenty-five years, (inftead of *thirty pounds*, its utmoft value at prefent,) be worth *one hundred and ten pounds* at leaft, after allowing *ten pounds* for the injury thefe referves or overftands may do to fome of the coppice wood.

Now, fuppofing forty only of thefe referves to be felled at the expiration of twenty-five years, and forty of the new growth to be then marked to fupply their places, the value of the fecond fall, *viz.* in fifty years from this year, might be eftimated as follows, at the loweft calculation:

	£.	s.	d.
The coppice wood,	20	0	0
Forty referves of fifty years growth, at one guinea each,	45	10	0
Forty ditto, of feventy-five years growth, *five pounds* each at an avarage.	200	0	0
	£265	10	0
Add to the above the value of the firft fall, deducting forty guineas for forty of the fifty year old referves, which are fuppofed to be ftill left at this fall,	64	10	0
The value of the acre in fifty years, will then amount to	£330	0	0

And

account, most interested, viz. the the management of natural woods or plantations, at the time when they are in general considered *fit for felling ;*

And this great encrease of the profit of our woods, obtained simply by the allowance of *four pounds* per acre, at the first sale of the coppice, out of its present value, that being the average of what the wood-buyer could demand, for leaving eighty reserves on the acre, and often much more than he would charge, as he is thus saved the expence of manufacturing them. I well know, that the *lovers* of *money,* which I am sorry to say, is a term too often synonymous to the *enemies* of *Timber,* will ask, what might be made of *four pounds* put out to interest in fifty years ? I will allow for argument sake, though I am sure it is four times more than any of my brother planters, or wood-owners have ever made, or are likely to make of it, that by *compound* interest, it may arrive to the enormous sum, in proportion, of *one hundred and twenty-eight pounds*; but even that deducted from *three hundred and thirty pounds,* leaves a sum of *two hundred and two pounds* net profit by the acre, and that gained not by incessant toil, anxious parsimoney, and subject to perpetual risque, but with certainty, in a great measure without the least exertion, and I might say, without the necessity of even a *thought* on the subject, if not entered into for our own gratification and amusement; when we shall have the pleasure of finding in this mode of managing our woods and coppices, that what in the end must prove

ling; and here I muſt obſerve, that few things have been more prejudicial to the landed intereſt of Ireland, than the abſurd opinion adopted about forty-years ſince with reſpect to woods, *viz.* that wherever a wood was *felled*, it was uſeleſs, if not detrimental, to leave a *ſingle reſerve*, and that no ſhoot from a tree, once cut down, could ever grow to *timber*.

This ill founded theory ſtripped whole counties at once, both of their ornament and ſhelter: whereas a judicious *thinning-fall*, repeated from time to time, wou'd have kept up that appearance of woodland which we remark in almoſt every ſhire in England; and would at the ſame time have produced within a very few years, as is already ſtated, an infinitely greater profit than the advocates of a *general fall* could ever hope for, at their higheſt calculation, and even with com-

---

prove a ſource of wealth to our family, contributes in the meantime, to ſome of the moſt refined and rational enjoyments of life, whilſt in the words of the truly paſtoral Shenſtone,

We "*Call forth refreſhing Shades, and decorate Repoſe.*"

pound

pound intereft to affift them, as may evidently appear from the ftatement in the preceding note.

We find among other pieces of valuable information, for which we are much indebted to the intelligent author of " Minutes of Agriculture and Planting, in the midland Shires of England," that four acres of oak in Warwick-Shire, of about fixty-four years growth, has paid already by various thinnings above *four hundred pounds*. That the referved timber trees, (which are now confidered as ftanding too clofe) are worth from twenty to twenty-five fhillings each, the foil a hungry deep clay, of no greater value than *feven fhillings and fix pence* per acre.

Now, fuppofing the over-ftands at this time to be only forty on each acre, and taken at the loweft valuation, viz. twenty fhillings each, the return of the acre from paft falls, and prefent value of timber, amounts to *one hundred and forty pounds*, and would on the *Irifh* acre in fimilar circumftances, amount to *two hundred and ten pounds*, which at *ten fhillings* for the

value

value of the land, (a rate at which many thousand acres capable of producing valuable timber, might be rented in this kingdom), is *four hundred and twenty* years purchafe and that within *feventy* years at moft. †

---

† It gave me great pleafure to find that the calculation I had made of the value of an acre of wood, properly managed, with well chofen referves, amounting at the third fall to the net fum of *two hundred and two pounds*, fhould be fo ftrongly fupported by the above return, of the actual produce of the four acres in Warwickfhire; in addition to which, I find in an ingenious treatife communicated to the Secretary of the Bath Society, by a gentleman in Norfolk, that a particular oak, which meafured in 1768, feven feet eight inches round, in 1771 was eight feet, and in 1790, was ten feet in circumference: from this he argues, that after the firft twenty-five or thirty years, no tree grows fafter than the oak, in a foil properly fuited to it; extending yearly about one inch and one-third in circumference; but this growth caufing an encreafe in the quantity of timber in *a geometrical proportion*. So that admitting, in 1768, that the tree contained one hundred and ten feet of timber, in 1790, it contained two hundred feet; thus encreafing ninety feet of timber in twenty-two years.—This proves to demonftration, the great progreffive value of oak from fifty to one hundred years ftanding: after *that age* I am not enabled to determine, whether or not they attain any confiderable encreafe either in *bulk* or *value*.

As to the danger of the reserved trees decaying, there is not the least room for apprehension, if not left *too thin* at the first fall, or injudiciously marked out of such trees, as have grown in *thick clusters*, in preference to those that have stood *single* for some time, and gained an ascendancy over the surrounding plants. Every copice wood contains a sufficiency of such trees as those latter, to be made choice of for *reserves*; and as to their future growth, it is now incontestably proved, that some of the finest trees which England has produced, have arisen from old stools. I have in my own woods, an oak of this description, growing in two stems from the root, which is worth at least twelve guineas, and there is another in the domain of Ballybeg, in this neighbourhood, which measures round the forked trunk upwards of *twenty-seven* feet, round one of the stems *twenty* feet, and round the other *twelve*, and is grofs timber for more than *forty* feet in height, as we shall see more particularly hereafter.

This last has the honour of being one of the few remaining trees of those woods, which rendered the barony of Shillela, in the county of Wicklow,

Wicklow, proverbially famous for its timber, and gave the denomination of *Fairwood-Park* to that diſtrict in which the great, but unfortunate Earl of Stafford built his hunting-lodge. His deſcendant, Earl Fitzwilliam now poſſeſſes this eſtate, from whoſe liberal attention to whatever may in any way promote the benefit of this country*, and from the excellent ſyſtem adopted by the gentlemen who have the preſent management of his Lordſhip's woods, I flatter myſelf that poſterity may ſee Shillela as remarkable, for timber in the next century, as in the laſt, when its oak, if we may judge from the ſpecimens which ſtill remain, was as ſuperior to moſt others in the firmneſs of its texture, as in its ſtately height and great dimenſions. An inſtance of the latter has fallen within my knowledge, too

---

* His Lordſhip has expended within theſe two years, above 4000l. in building a Hall for the ſale of coarſe woollen goods, which are made to great perfection in the neighbourhood of Rathdrum. He might have been aſſiſted by a large ſubſcription in this truly uſeful work, but generouſly determined to carry it on, at his own expence.

remark-

remarkable to be paffed over in a treatife, which profeffes to enforce the important object of referving a certain portion of our woods, for the ufe of pofterity.

Some years fince the late Mr. Siffon, who was employed as a mafter-builder, under the furveyor-general of public works, having laid out confiderable fums in the purchafe of timber on the Shillela eftate, was defired by the then agent to chufe one tree for his own ufe, as a compliment to him for the preference he had given to thofe woods in the courfe of his employment. He made choice of an oak, which though *forked* from the ground, was of fuch dimenfions that each ftem was grofs enough for a *mill-fhaft* at more than *fifty feet* from the but. Two pieces were appropriated to that ufe, the remainder he fawed into very thin pannels, which fold from the faw by meafurement, for upwards of 250*l.* He might have taken a larger tree, but prefer'd this, on account of the ftraightnefs of the ftem and clearnefs of the grain; from which circumftances, and its being *forked*

(82)

from the ground, there is the utmoſt reaſon to believe, that this great maſs of timber proceeded from the root of a tree which had once been felled, though in all probability at *no advanced* age.*

But ſuppoſing that the poſſibility of having a fine growth of timber from the *old ſtools* could not be as fully proved, as it is now allow-

---

* I have the ſatisfaction of finding this ſtatement of the great value of the tree felled by Mr. Siſſon, ſupported by the accurate return of the produce of the Langley oak on the verge of the new foreſt in Hampſhire, with which Mr. T. South, of Baſſington, has favoured the Bath Society.

The tree was felled in the year 1758; its branches, which contained knees fit for a firſt rate ſhip, extended forty feet on every ſide; its trunk which was about twenty feet high, meaſured twelve feet diameter at the ground, and ſix feet at the top; the contents of the whole amounted to thirty-two load of hewn timber, which at half-a-crown per foot, produced preciſely *two hundred pounds*.—It is ſtated by Mr. South, that an oak of ſixty years growth, will in twenty-four years from that period, double its contents of timber, which I conſider a very valuable piece of information.

ed

ed to be, in the opinion of several of the most experienced persons, in the management of woods: What is there to prevent a sufficiency of *saplins* from the *acorn* which are to be found in almost every coppice, from coming to the utmost perfection, if suffered to remain and carefully attended to? I have seen such saplins promising to supply the *requisite quantity of future timber*, though every tree in the coppice which had once been felled, should be cut again at every fall. The loss to several estates by this indiscriminate destruction of the *entire growth* at every twenty or twenty-five years as *mere underwood*, is not to be conceived by those who have not had experience of the advantage resulting from a contrary practice. I am happy at being able to confirm what I advance by a very strong instance, in my own neighbourhood. An estimate was made in one thousand seven hundred and eighty-seven, by the direction of Colonel Symes, of the value of his woods, at Ballyarthur, near Arklow. The timber stands on about one hundred and forty acres, exclusive of some hedgerows; the oldest trees did not much exceed one hundred years growth, and of these there were but few: the second rate had stood about eighty years, and the youngest over-stands about fifty; the rest were mere coppice wood, but which had grown in general pretty well under the reserves; an evident proof that these latter stood at a considerable distance from each other, and did not nearly occupy the whole of the ground; the present Proprietor's father freely cut the underwood at *stated periods*; religiously reserving the old timber, or an adequate quantity of the best of the young growth, to succeed such overstands, as were occasionally felled for particular purposes: This self-denying attention to his timber, which from the habit of managing woods in that neighbourhood, in a very different manner, was looked upon at the time, as rather *injurious*, than *advantageous* to his property, and the result of whim rather than of judgment, was amply repaid to his family, when, a very few years after his death, on the estimate above mentioned, the woods on the domain were valued to *fourteen thousand five hundred pounds*, at which rate, the valuator offered to become a purchaser of the whole or any part. From the

the abfence of Colonel Symes at this * moment in the fervice of his country, as indeed has been the cafe during the greater part of his life, I am unable to ftate the particular value of each of the former falls, † but I have fufficient grounds to affert, that at the time of making the above valuation, the wood which had been felled on the domain within fifty years, had produced three times the value of the fee fimple of the ground it occupied.

---

* At Newport in Flanders, when this was written.

† It will be a pleafure to the lovers of old timber, to learn, that there ftill remains on the eftate above *ten thoufand pounds* worth of wood, not likely to be cut till an ample fucceeding growth fhall give full fanction to its fall.

NOR need the planter wait the regular returns of his coppice woods, for the reward of his attention, it may be almoſt daily repaid him by a ſkilful management. The judicious woodman, whilſt he leaves the beſt of each ſtool for future uſe, knows how to turn the ſmalleſt branches to advantage; the thinnings of our coppices, or of our plantations, which have run up too much for tranſplantation, anſwer according to their ſize for ſeveral purpoſes of rural oeconomy; for building, partitioning, and roofing farm houſes or cottages, for railing, upright paling, or ſtakes for hedges: Birch and alder of the ſmalleſt ſize will ſell for the chairmakers uſe; if larger, they are uſed for cart ſaddles, foals for pattens, and heels for women's ſhoes, the demand for which is often very conſiderable.

Slender aſh poles are valuable for hoops, ſpade, and pitchfork handles, rakes tails, and garden eſpaliers: if a little *groſſer*, and ſomewhat *crooked* they make the beſt plow handles, horſe hames, and ſwingle trees, and if ever ſo crooked and knotty, may be, not only *uſeful*, but *ornamental*

in

Plate II. P 87.

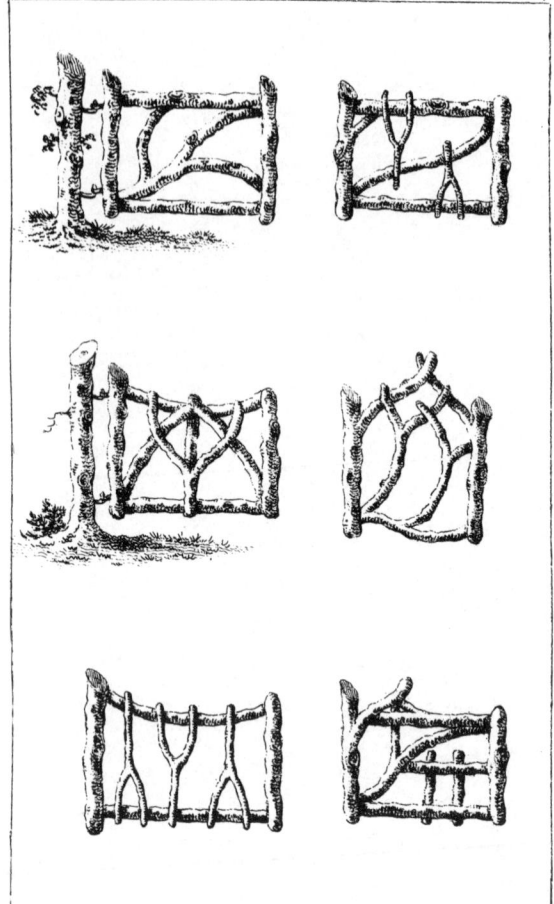

in ruſtic buildings, gates,* and paling. The fallow is not only adapted to the above purpoſes, but from its durability and lightneſs, is particularly excellent for making ſheep bars, or moveable fences, uſually called in England flatted hurdles; † if too ſmall for that uſe, it may be wrought up as well as the hazel into hoops, laceing of ſtake hedges, or binding for their tops, as the rim of a baſket is uſually finiſhed, which will make them laſt ſeveral years; ‡ they are uſed alſo for cloſe wrought hurdles for penning ſheep, or into a ſort of net-work hurdle for that purpoſe, very light and durable when well made, of which I have given a ſketch, as not being much known in this kingdom. The ſmalleſt fallow and hazel anſwer for baſkets, or to form little cribs or low ſheep racks, preferred in many parts of England, to thoſe of a more expenſive conſtruction, as being free from two imperfections, viz. that of *cauſing the graſs ſeed* to fall into the *ſheep's wool*, and producing a cold

---

* *Vide* Plate II. and IV. † *Vide* Plate III. Fig. 1.
‡ *Vide* Plate III. Fig. 2. § *Vide* Plate IV. Fig. 1.

draft

draft of air, to the *legs* and *breaſt* of the animal, where they are moſt fuſceptible of injury from the weather.*

The thinnings of our *oak woods,* though leſs durable than any of the preceeding when cut young, and in full ſap, which is always the caſe from the value of the *bark* at that time, are not only of uſe for moſt of the purpoſes before mentioned when ſtraight, but if a little crooked, are to be preferred to any others for poling of hops, whoſe bells ripen better on vines which hang looſely from three ſuch poles, at the uſual diſtance at bottom, but with their tops bending *outwards,* than when ſtraighter and ſmoother timber is uſed for the purpoſe.

If very *crooked* and *knotty,* they may be wrought up like the cankard aſh before-mentioned, unto ſeveral ſorts of paling, ruſtic gates, ſeats, wood-houſes and other picturefque buildings, ſuch as the few deſigns annexed, may give ſome

---

* *Vide* Plate III. Figure 3.

idea

Plate III.   P.88

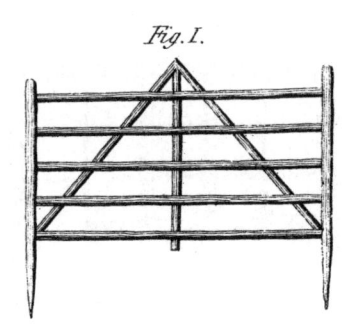

Fig. I.

Fig. II.

Fig. III.

Plate IV.

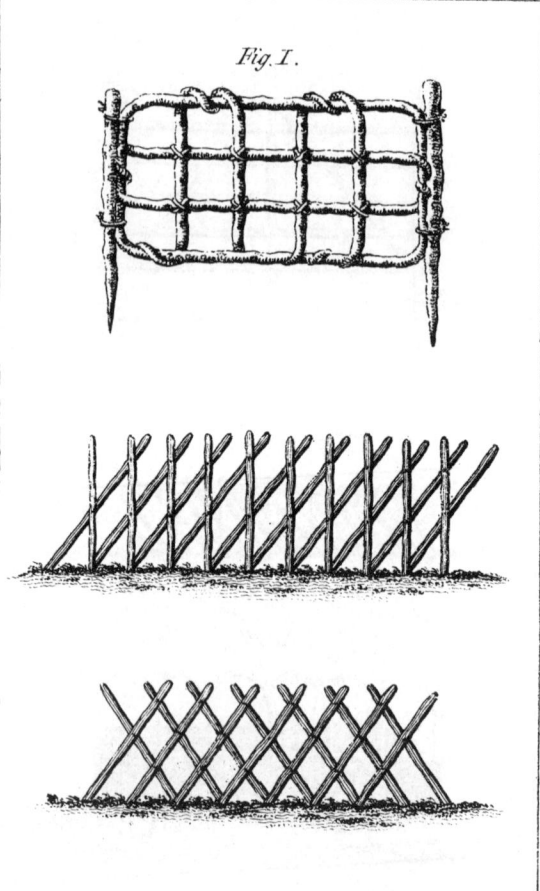

Fig. I.

idea of; † the laſt purpoſes to which I think the thinnings of plantations and coppices to be applied to, is firewood and charcoal, though the latter is a very ſaleable commodity; it is on the whole the leaſt deſirable uſe to which timber can be converted, as no country ever ſo well wooded, can long ſtand the depredation made by furnaces, which are to be ſupplied with wood alone as their conſtant fuel.

Thus what we thin out of our woods or coppices of every ſize and ſhape, may be converted to uſeful purpoſes, with conſiderable profit at the preſent, and at the ſame time to the advantage of the future growth, as I may venture from experience to affirm, that the oftener a thick coppice is judiciouſly thin'd, the greater will be its value in twenty-five years, at which time I ſuppoſe the whole to be fell'd, except the *reſerves* for future timber.

---

† *Vide* Vignette,

The number of thefe muft in a great meafure depend on the circumftances of their paſt growth, and the expofure of the ground on which they ſtand; if they have not grown well and are in a bleak fituation, about *one hundred* fhould be left on the acre, but if their growth has been advanced by proper thinning, a greater fhelter or a richer foil, *fixty* or *eighty* will be fully fufficient.—This quantity to the Irifh acre coincides very nearly with what Mr. Evelyn directs fhould be left on the Englifh, in order to maintain a conftant fucceffion; viz. four of the beft growth, fourteen fecond beft, fourteen thirds, and eight wavers or young faplins; and fo attentive were our Englifh anceſtors to infure a proper fupply of timber, that the proprietors of woods were compelled by the ftatute of the thirty-fifth of Henry the Eighth, to leave twelve of the beft *ſtandrils* on every acre of coppice at each fall, together with a due proportion of a younger growth for fucceffion; and were, at the fame time reſtricted from cutting any of the former, 'till they fhould meafure

forty

forty inches in circumference, at five feet from the ground.*

---

* It is to be regretted that fimilar regulations with refpect to woods were not enacted in this kingdom, at the time of the introduction of the tenth of William the Third, which as the preamble fets forth, was intended to provide againft the great wafte of timber, caufed by the ravages of civil war, and the introduction of iron forges and furnaces. This ftatute for enforcing the annual plantation of a certain number of trees, in proportion to the ground which each proprietor occupied, was not attended with the good confequences expected, and which the above regulations would in a great meafure have produced; as the feveral circumftances of foil and fituation, together with competent fkill, and continual attention, which were all requifite in one cafe, by no means applied to the other. That fuch regulations were wanting is a melancholy truth, too evident to every perfon who travels through this kingdom, and confequently fees what tracts of wood have been laid wafte by tenants for life of all defcriptions, who fo far from leaving *referves*, are feldom at the pains even of fencing up the young coppice, for the advantage of their fucceffors.—Amongft many other inftances, I am forry, I am obliged to ftate, that I have been eye-witneffes to the fall of nearly two hundred acres of beautiful well growing oak, in a romantic valley, on the fee lands

To be enabled to purfue this excellent method, the utmoſt care ſhould be obſerved in felling coppices in ſuch a manner, as may enſure

---

of Glandelough in the county of Wicklow, *three times* within the ſpace of *twenty-four* years—the produce of each ſale to the ſeveral Archbiſhops never exceeded one hundred pounds, and as I am informed, amounted once only to *fifty pounds*, or *five ſhillings* per acre for a coppice, which had it only been preſerved for the ſame number of years, though not containing a ſingle *reſerve* of a former growth, would have produced *thirty pounds* per acre at the loweſt valuation, or *ſix thouſand pounds* in place of *fifty*.

I am far from wiſhing that any individual or body of men, and leaſt of all at this time, that the *church* ſhould be deprived of the ſmalleſt portion of their rights and property, but I am certain, that means might be deviſed to remedy this evil, without any ſuch conſequence: the value of thoſe woods, which belong to tenants for life, corporate bodies, &c. and ſuch as are not fit for a *general fall*, might be taken at *ſtated periods*, and the amount of the whole, or ſuch reſerves as ſhall be required to ſtand, together with intereſt from that time, charged on the *ſucceſſor*, whoſe future property may be conſidered as ſo far *mortgaged* for the diſcharge of that ſum in the firſt inſtance.—The tenant for life, in this caſe can be no

loſer,

sure a sound and perfect growth from the stools, and such as might hereafter afford a choice of young trees for future reserves, if there should not be found a sufficiency of *saplins from the acorns.*—There is a wide difference of opinion on this subject; I have known some

owners

---

loser, whilst the successor and the nation at large, will be benefited by a valuable growth of timber, and that in a degree so disproportionate to what can arise from the sale of such miserable premature falls as I allude to, that I shall be pardoned the warmth of expression by all lovers of timber, and the improvement of their country, when I assert, that a contrary conduct tho' continued for so many years, could only have originated in the *grossest ignorance, and unenlightened avarice*; at the same time, I have the pleasure of observing, that the late act, which gives to the *tenant* the profit of such woodland on his farm, as he may fence up for coppice at his own expence, subject to certain restrictions, has been attended in many places with all the advantages expected from the measure; amongst other instances, a very confiderable tract of the above woods of Glandelough, have been fenced up from cattle by James Chritchly, Esq. a tenant of the See of Dublin, with the present Archbishop's approbation, and the wood is now in a fine growing state.

owners of large tracts of wood, and great lovers of timber, who have cautiously prohibited the stripping of bark off their oak nearer than *six* inches to the ground, about which spot they suppose the tree to be felled, whilst others wish to have the bark stripped as near the ground as possible, provided that in so doing, there is no part whatever of the root laid bare.

I profess to be of the last opinion, and think the advocates for the former method, would on closer investigation, save themselves a deal of unnecessary trouble to little purpose at best, if not to their considerable injury; as it must be evident to any person, who will give himself the trouble of examining the growth of a shoot from an old stock, that so long as the sap has a portion of bark to ascend through, the shoot is not forced out; but at last makes its appearance at some inches above the ground, on the side of the old stub, and often in a horizontal position; where if several weak ones are thus produced, they form an unsightly tuft of almost useless brush-wood; but if one by superior strength,

ſtrength, or by the others being pruned away, ſhall take a lead, it muſt be by bending upwards at its baſe, like a breaſt quick in a ditch, with this difference in favour of the latter, that the one depends immediately on its own roots, whilſt the young oak has nothing to depend on but the ſhell of the old ſtub, which in this ſituation generally becomes rotten within ſide, and daily leſs and leſs able to give that ſupport, which the encreaſing weight of the young tree is daily more in need of: from this circumſtance, it happens, that we ſo often find ſome of our talleſt young oak, from ten to fifteen years growth, lying flat on the ground in our coppices, *ſlip'd off* as it were, from the old ſtool at the ſpot from whence they were produced; whereas if the bark had been ſtrip'd quite to the ground, and the tree then cut as low as poſſible with a ſharp axe, leaving the center of the ſtub a little higher than the edges, the young ſhoots muſt have ſprung up like *ſuckers*, quite free from the original ſtem, and often at ſix or eight inches diſtance from it, their buts being ſufficiently low in the
ground

ground to enable them to ſtrike roots for themſelves, and ſtanding at ſuch a diſtance from each other, that their growth may be perpendicular for ſeveral years without interference, and conſequently till they arrive at ſuch a ſize that the worſt may be felled for uſeful purpoſes, and the beſt *reſerved*, with nearly the ſame advantage as if it had been a *ſapling* produced from the acorn.

The better to explain what I have defcribed, as the refult of the different methods of ftripping off the bark, I have added a fketch of three coppice oaks,* two of them growing in the way we fhould wifh to prevent, and the third in fuch a manner as to promife a good ftock of coppice wood, or even future timber if properly thin'd, and attended to in its growth.

Senfible at the fame time, of the bad confequence of having any part of the root ftripped of its bark, I have generally employed an intelligent labourer to attend the workmen, who *precede* the *fellers*, and whofe bufinefs it is to take off that part of the bark, which would otherwife be chopped into ufelefs pieces by the axe: he fhould fee that a cut is given all round the ftem, juft above the ground, which will ftop the ftripping of the bark at that fpot; he muft alfo take care that no injury is done to thofe trees which are *marked* to ftand as *referves*; this, with the appointment

---

* *Vide* vignette preceding.

pointment of another careful person to watch that the fellers cut smooth, and do not leave the stub hollow in the middle, which is technically termed *dishing* by the woodmen, will ensure a fine healthy growth; at the same time, by furnishing this latter with a long pole as before described, by which he may draw towards him or push off the falling tree, so as best to escape the reserves, we shall find the advantages will amply repay the expence of their wages; especially as the season of felling oak is confined to a few weeks in summer.

Though I know many valuable coppices at this moment, on which no farther care has been bestowed than what I have above mentioned, and that of being carefully preserved from cattle, without which no future growth can ever be expected, * Yet, I have little doubt, of the

great

---

* The vigorous growth of grass during the first three years after the felling of a wood, renders a coppice a continual object of trespass to every beast, and I may almost say, to every owner of a beast in its vicinity:
along

great advantage which might follow the application of Mr. Forefyth's compofition; efpecially where it is found neceffary to fell *one or more* plants off the fame ftool, on which we mean to leave a *referve*.

The teftimonies in favour of his practice are fo numerous, and highly refpectable, that I regret I have

---

along with the grafs, they devour the young growth of trees; and the temptation of fuch a quantity of pafturage is fo ftrong, that it is hardly poffible to find a coppice-keeper of fufficient integrity to withftand it.—A ftout difintcrefted wood-ranger is a moft valuable fervant, and deferves every poffible encouragement: moft owners of woods are much in their coppice-keepers power—I have known fome weak enough to take the advice of a felfifh knave, and fell all their woods without *referves*, leaft thefe latter might *decay*; when the true motive for giving fuch advice, was merely to avoid the *trouble* of having them under his care, and that there might be *more grafs* in the wood, in confequence of the overftands being cut down; others are affured, and implicitly believe it, that horfes do no injury to young trees, and in confequence give their wood-rangers privilege to keep a few horfes in their coppices, of which they take care to avail themfelves to their own *great emolument*, and the *deftruction* of their mafter's woods.

I have not had time sufficient to enable me to recommend it from my own experience.

What I had made use of before I heard of Mr. Foresyth's composition, when an application of that nature seemed necessary, was a sort of Dutch grafting wax or mummy. Tho' the ingredients are more expensive, and the method of applying it more troublesome, yet as I have known it used with great success on considerable wounds, given to peach, plumb and cherry trees,†

and

---

† A few years since, a great mastiff dog slip'd into my garden, just before the gardener quitted it for the night. The dog was no sooner locked in, than the animal became impatient of his situation, and made incessant efforts to regain his liberty; the consequence was, that in attempting during the whole night to get over a twelve foot wall, and fastening his feet continually in the wall trees, as he fell back he tore several of them almost to pieces; they were at that moment in high bearing, and covered with fruit.—The gardener's feelings on this occasion when he entered in the morning, may be easily conceived; there was no remedy, but patiently to prune off the broken branches, some of which were very large, and cover the wounds with the grafting

and those in the middle of summer, I shall copy the receipt for making it,‡ as well as that published

---

ing wax above mentioned, they were soon healed, fine fresh wood was produced. and many of the trees are now in better order, than before the accident happened.

‡ Directions for making the Dutch Grafting Wax:

"Take one pound of common black pitch, a quarter of a pound of common turpentine, put them together into an earthen pot, and set it on fire in the air, holding a cover ready to quench it with, which must be done suddenly, and repeated several times.—This prepared pitch must then have a quantity of bees wax added to it 'till it is of a proper confiftency.

"N. B. It should be put on as warm as it can be used without injury to the wood or bark of the tree, on this fine sand may be sifted, which will prevent the Sun from having any effect on it."

Directions for the medicated Tar, used with great success in dressing of the wounds of orchard trees, as communicated to the Society of Arts, &c. &c. in London, by Thomas S. D. Bucknell, Esq.

"Take a quarter of an ounce of corrosive sublimate, reduced to fine powder, by beating with a wooden mallet,

lifhed by Mr. Forefyth, ‖ and think there may be particular circumſtances where the application

---

" mallet, put it into a three pint earthen pipkin, with a
" glafs of ſtrong ſpirits, and ſtir it well together, till the
" ſublimate is diſſolved : the veſſel is then to be filled
" with common tar, and ſtirred 'till the whole mixture
" is well blended."—The above quantity is ſufficient for dreſſing two hundred apple trees.

‖ Directions for making a Compoſition for curing difeaſes, defects and injuries, in all kinds of fruit and foreſt trees, and the method of preparing the trees, and laying on the Compoſition, by Mr. William Forefyth, of Kenfington, as delivered in on oath to the Land Revenue Office Scotland-yard, London, the 11th of May, 1791 :

" Take one buſhel of freſh cow dung, half a buſhel
" of lime rubbiſh of old buildings, that from the ciel-
" ing of rooms is preferable, half a buſhel of wood-
" aſhes, and one-ſixteenth part of a buſhel of pit or river
" fand, the three laſt articles are to be ſifted fine be-
" fore they are mixed ; then work them together with
" a ſpade, and afterwards with a wooden beater, until
" the ſtuff is very ſmooth, like fine plaiſter uſed for the
" cielings of rooms."

" The compoſition being thus made, care muſt be
" taken to prepare the tree properly for its application,
" by

cation of one might be attended with advantages,

"by cutting away all the dead, decayed and injured part, 'till you come to the fresh sound wood, leaving the surface of the wood very smooth, and rounding off the edges of the bark with a draw knife, or other instrument perfectly smooth, which must be particularly attended to; then lay on the plaister about an eighth of an inch thick, all over the part where the wood or bark has been so cut away, finishing off the edges as thin as possible: then take a quantity of dry powder of wood ashes, mixed with one-sixth part of the same quantity of burnt bones; put it into a tin box with holes at the top, and shake the powder on the surface of the plaister, till the whole is covered over with it, letting it remain for half an hour to absorb the moisture; then apply more powder, rubbing it on gently with the hand, and repeating the application of the powder, 'till the whole plaister becomes a dry, smooth surface.

"All trees cut down near the ground should have the surface made quite smooth, rounding it off in a small degree, as before mentioned, and the dry powder directed to be used afterwards, should have an equal quantity of powder of alabaster mixed with it, in order the better to resist the dripping of trees and heavy rains.

"Any

tages, which could not fo well refult from the other.§

"Any of the compofition not ufed muft be kept in
"a veffel, covered with urine of any kind, or the at-
"mofphere will injure the efficacy of the application;
"where lime, rubbifh of old buildings cannot be got,
"pounded chalk, or common lime after being flacked
"one month at leaft, will anfwer.

"As the growth of the tree difturbs the plaifter on
"the edges next the bark, that part fhould be rubbed
"over with the finger after rain, to fmooth down the
"plaifter, and keep it whole, to prevent air and wet
"from getting into the wound."

§ Where the application may be wanting to a torn root, or when it may be thought neceffary to cover the ends of tender cuttings, the grafting wax feems more likely to anfwer the purpofe, than Mr. Forefyth's compofition. By the application of the wax to the fmalleft cuttings pof- fible, and covering them with a cap glafs, I have foon found them rooted plants: where they have been as large as a walking-ftick, I have fet them quite perpen- dicular, in a rich fhady border, in which fituation they have thrown out vigorous branches from the top, and the cutting has become a fmooth ftem. I have raifed many handfomer plants of the common or Portugal laurel in this way, than ever I faw from the *berries* and that in one third of the time, as I plant the cuttings from three to five feet high.

GREAT ASH OF LEIX.
S.H. del.

ON THE

MAGNITUDE, VALUE

And QUICKNESS of GROWTH of

SEVERAL

TREES IN IRELAND.

HAVING in the beginning of this little essay instructed the *Planter* to the best of my ability, in the different methods he may pursue for the attainment of a valuable growth of wood, and now inculcated to the *proprietors of woodland*, the absolute necessity of attention to their trees and coppices whilst young, and of *reserving* a certain portion of the best grown plants at every fall, (if only for *their own* emolument not to mention the advantage of such a process to *posterity*). I can in no way

P better

better support whatever arguments I may have advanced in favour of *planting* and *reserving of timber*, than by enumerating those instances of great magnitude and value to which many trees have arrived in this kingdom; together with such specimens of a quick growth, as have either fallen within my immediate observation, or have been so well authenticated that I can vouch for their truth. The *one*, must naturally inculcate the preservation of timber, whilst the *other* cannot fail of stimulating the *active* and *spirited* Planter to *double* his exertions, and may encourage the most *timid* to *persevere*.

Such has been the waste of timber in Ireland during the last century from the unsettled state of the kingdom, and other causes, amongst which we may reckon the introduction of iron forges and furnaces, that there scarcely exists in some districts, a sufficiency to favour the supposition, that we ever possessed a valuable growth; but from what I have seen I am inclined to believe, that on an attentive survey, we should find a far greater number of trees of considerable dimensions

dimensions *now standing*, than a traveller could suppose on a cursory view of the country.

It was at first my intention to have undertaken this general survey; but finding that it would have been attended with more trouble and delay than at first appeared, I confined my enquiries to a few neighbouring counties; the result, which I think very satisfactory, I shall have the pleasure of communicating: Except in a few instances I kept entirely to the maritime side of the county of Wicklow, Queen's county and the county of Dublin, and even in these, I must have left several trees unnoticed, which no doubt deserved attention.

I could have considerably enlarged my catalogue, if I had not determined to state nothing which may not be perfectly relied on, and even thus, the instances I am enabled to give of the great trees still standing, or whose remains are sufficient to authenticate what they were within a few years, are fully adequate to prove, that Ireland in due time is capable of producing timber of the *first magnitude;* and that consequently we can never be too careful of the *woods* we *already possess*; whilst the several specimens of rapid growth I can adduce, will be found sufficient on the other hand to encourage the *Planter* to extend his labours as I before observed to the utmost of his ability; not only as a healthy and rational amusement, and for the purpose of ornamenting his domain, but as a profitable employment, a source of future wealth to his family, and (if he makes *oak* his choice, as no doubt it ought, whether we consider the *bark** or the *timber*) as intimately connected

---

* So great is the deficiency of oak bark at this time in Ireland in proportion to the demand, that the Chancellor of our Exchequer Sir John Parnel, from that attention to the manufactures of this kingdom which he (as well as his predecessor in office the present peaker,) has been long known to possess, was induced to propose in the last sessions a bounty of three shillings per barrel on all bark imported into the kingdom during the current year. This measure may at first appear injurious to that spirit of *planting*, which as an extensive Planter himself, and on many other considerations, the Chancellor of the Exchequer would certainly wish to encourage; but exclusive of several countervailing circumstances, such as a large additional

nected with the advancement of the manufactures and general improvement of his country.

---

additional bounty on *oak plantations,* &c. which the Dublin Society have in contemplation to offer, it is, I believe, a fact, that the *bark* of no other country (England excepted, who does not wish to export it) will ever be purchased by our manufacturers, when *that of our own can be procured.* I shall take an opportunity of enlarging more hereafter on this subject.

ON THE

MAGNITUDE and VALUE of TREES.

IN the small survey, which as before mentioned, my time permitted me to make, the district of *Shillela* in the county of Wicklow first claimed my attention. Though the name, with little variation in the spelling, may be literally tranflated *fair-wood*, there are *few* now remaining of those celebrated oak which authorized that denomination; but those *few* are sufficient to support what has been handed down to us concerning them —Tradition gives the *Shillela Oak* the honor of roofing Westminster-Hall and other buildings of that age; the timbers which support the leads of the magnificent chapel of King's College Cambridge, which was built in 1444, as also the roof of Henry VIII[th's] chapel in Westminster-abbey, are said to be of oak brought from these woods, and I think it by no means improbable, that the superior density and closeness of grain which is the character of the *Irish Oak*, particularly in high situations and a dry soil, as may appear by comparing its specific gravity with that of other Oak, added to the inattention of

the

the Irish at that time to the article of *bark*, which permitted their oak to be felled in winter, when *free from sap*, might have induced the English Architects to give it the preference in such material works; and it must be allowed that the present unimpaired state of these roofs, after so many centuries, seems very well to warrant this conjecture.

It is generally understood that a sale was made of some of the finest Timber of *Shillela* which remained in Charles II.'s time, into Holland for the use of the Stadt-house and other buildings, constructed on piles driven close together to the number of several hundred thousand. In 1669 William Earl of Strafford furnished Laurence Wood of London with such pipe staves, to a great amount at 10*l. per thousand* as are now sold for *fifty*, and are only to be had from *America*. The year 1692 introduced into *Shillela* that bane of all our timber, *iron forges and furnaces;* and as the parties were allowed to fell for themselves several thousand cord of wood yearly, and were only confined to a particular district, they

cut

cut whatever was moſt convenient to them for the purpoſe, and it is inconceivable what deſtruction they muſt have made in the courſe of *twenty years* which was the term of their contract. I find by a memorandum in my poſſeſſion relative to ſome of my own woods, that in 1666 many thouſand cord of wood ſold at 4*d.* *per* cord which now ſells on the ſame ground for 7*s.* 6*d.* however the iron works left ſome very noble trees ſtill ſtanding, as we ſee by the ſale of Mr. *Siſſon's* tree before mentioned, which produced two large mill-ſhafts, and upwards of 200*l.* for the remainder of the timber when ſawed into coach pannels; and it alſo appears from a paper in the hand-writing of *Thomas Marquis of Rockingham*, found amongſt the papers of his ſon the late *Marquis of Rockingham* (who to his numerous amiable qualities and endowments, added a great knowledge of rural œconomics, as we find not only from the management of his grounds and the deſire he manifeſted of improving the huſbandry of his neighbourhood*, ſo ably communicated

---

* The deſire of improving the agriculture of the country round him as mentioned by Mr. Young, was

not

nicated by Mr. Young, but from several minutes of agriculture which I have seen of his own writing) that in 1731 there were standing in that

---

not confined to his estate in England, the same patriotic attention was extended to this kingdom in a variety of ways; he gave 500l. to purchase arms for a loyal and spiritedbody of his tenantry who formed a volunteer association in 1779, at the moment of an expected invasion; about the year following he sent over the old *Kentish farmer*, (whose plough and general management is so much applauded by Mr. Young) to instruct such of the tenants as might wish to follow his practice: several of the implements of husbandry he introduced were found to be of singular service, and have since been adopted into very general use. When to these circumstances amongst many others of a similar nature, such as the grant of large sums to purchase provision for the poor in times of scarcity, and the liberal expenditure before-mentioned of Earl Fitzwilliam in building the Flannel-hall at *Rathdrum*, &c. we have to add, that there does not exist an instance of a single acre of the *Rockingham*, now *Fitzwilliam* estate having been ever *advertised* or offered to be let to the *best bidder*, but that his farm when out of lease is uniformly offered to the *tenant* at a fair valuation, we must allow that such *absentees* are in a great measure entitled to an exemption from that censure which others may have justly incurred; *these* leave us as little as possible *to regret in their absence*, but the *loss of their society*.

that part of *Shillela* called the *Deer Park* 2150 oak trees then valued at 8317*l*. the timber at 1*s*. 6*d*. per foot and the bark 7*s*. per barrel the fame trees at the rate thofe articles now fell for, would have produced at leaft 16,000*l*. One hundred and forty of thefe were marked to ftand for the future fupply of the machinery of the iron forges and furnaces before-mentioned, they were then valued at 511*l*. but as trees now fell were well worth 10*l*. *each* on an average: the remainder were not immediately cut down, for in 1737 there remained 1,540 trees; 1,400 of which were valued at the above low valuation to 6,000*l*. at the prefent value they would have been worth 9,800 or 7*l*. a tree one with another, which muft be allowed a very confiderable price for fuch a number.

In 1780 when Mr. Wainright Earl Fitzwilliam's prefent agent (to whofe obliging communication I am indebted for feveral of thefe particulars) arrived in this kingdom, there remained 38 only of the *old referves*, thefe had been valued two years before by Mr. Scot his Lordfhip's wood agent, (a gentleman eminently qualified for the office;) and he eftimated them to contain

2,588

2,588 feet of timber, which at the price fuch grofs timber would now fell for, together with the value of their bark, would make them worth 516*l.* for the 38 trees, or 13*l.* 10*s.* *each tree* on an average.—The evident fymptoms of decay which from that time they began to exhibit, owing to windfhakes and other diforders incidental to all old trees, who have loft a mafs of fhelter on every fide, made it expedient to cut them nearly all down from time to time; the *laſt* I remember to have been felled produced at three fhillings per foot 27l. 1s. 8d. another about the fame time was purchafed for the arm of a fire engine at Donane colliery, and with the rough end fawed off after the axe for which two guineas was given, produced 26*l.* 4*s.* 3*d.* there ftill remains one entire tree about 10 feet round at five feet from the ground, ftraight as a pine for 60 feet and about 6 feet round at that height; there is alfo in a little ifland in the forge pool a fhort trunk which meafures 21 feet round.

To succeed these however, there is a considerable number of healthy oak of a good growth for their age, in the adjoining woods of *Coolatin*, several of them about 7 feet 6 inches round with 30 feet or more of stem, and promising in time to be very fine trees, as well as some beautiful ash of a great height and 9 feet round; but the two best trees in the district of *Shillela* are in the domain of the Rev. Mr. Symes at *Ballybeg*, a very spirited Planter and great lover of trees; this is in the neighbourhood of those grounds, on which as I before observed, Thomas Earl of Strafford built his hunting lodge, by him called *Fairwood-Park*[*]; in these we have two objects well worth the attention of the arborist, one being an evident proof that coppiced

---

[*] It may amuse the Reader to see a description of this part of the country, at that period, and the manner in which he spent his time in it, in several of the letters of this truly *great*, but *unfortunate* man. In these letters which the ingenious Mr. Walpole has stiled *Chef d'œuvres of manly sense and eloquence*, he will also find a refutation of most of those calumnies and misrepresentations, under which the memory of their noble Author has very unwarrantably suffered.

piced trees are capable of growing to as great magnitude and value as can be defired; the other as an inftance of the very rapid growth of oak where the foil is well adapted to it—the firft which I have had occafion to mention before as growing on the bank of a ditch with a forked ftem evidently from an old ftool, is in the very *leaft* fpot in which it can be meafured 27 feet round, from whence the two ftems grow up very fair timber for a great height, one meafuring 20 feet round at the butt and 7 feet at 40 feet high, the other 12 feet at the butt and $5\frac{1}{2}$ feet round at the above height.

The fecond grows in a rich meadow nearer the garden and promifes in time to become one of the moft beautiful trees in Ireland, as its age does not exceed 80 years, and yet it is already 14 feet round at bottom and 12 at 8 feet high, the head in full health, finely formed, and extending *many yards* from the bole on every fide. Thefe two capital inftances fo perfectly in point with my fubject, one of the *great magnitude* to which a tree growing from the old ftool may arrive, and

the

the other of the *quick growth* of an oak where it likes the foil, muft plead my excufe with my brother Planters, if I have detained them too long in the woods of *Shillela*, and deviated in my detail fomewhat more into the habits of the *Antiquarian*, than may be allowable in a work of this nature.

There are fome confiderable Scots-fir at *Ballybeg* for their age, and at Mrs. Symes of *Hillbrook* not far from thence, many meafure 7 feet round at five feet from the ground, and 5 feet at 50 feet high; one felled in its 70th year was 77 feet fix inches in length of clear timber, and meafured 6 feet 6 inches round at 50 feet from the ground.

Shelton, the feat of Lord Vifcount Wicklow, near Arklow is finely wooded; we may fee there a witch elm 16 feet round at bottom and 15 feet 3 inches at 6 feet from the ground; feven beech whofe dimenfions are from 15 feet to 13 feet 9 inches round; and upwards of *fixty* from the laft fize to 10 feet round, many of thefe of

great

great height carrying the above girths for more than 40 *feet*.

The beech is not a native of Ireland; those at *Shelton* appear amongst the first which were brought into this kingdom, and from their mast, most of our finest beech have been propagated.

At the southern extremity of the domain of *Avondale* near *Rathdrum*, there is an oak standing, which though only fourteen feet round at five feet from the ground, was valued at more than 25*l.* before the year 1776. The head which was of very great height and extent, consisted of seven principal branches, each very grofs and finely formed for ship timber; a violent storm in the above year tore off four of them near the trunk, where they were about six feet round; this has greatly lessened the value of the tree, but from the vigorous growth and great height of the three remaining branches, which rise from the centre, it is still a fine object; and as the bark is now covering the parts

where

where the wounded branches were fawed off, I flatter myfelf, it may yet make a very confiderable tree.

The fame ftorm threw down a very fine old *Afh*, which grew nearly furrounded with water on the bank of the *Avonmore*, about one hundred yards from the *Oak*. The trunk, when fawed off the butt which ftill remains in the water, was above 14 feet round, and carried nearly the fame dimenfions for eighteen feet.— Of one plank I had a table made for my fervant's-hall, and though the tree had grown for many years full three parts in four of its ftem in water, it is by far the beft and firmeft wood of its kind I ever faw, of great weight, beautifully branched like mohogany, and capable of receiving a confiderable polifh; near this grew another remarkable *Afh* with a very lofty ftem and great head, but much covered with ivy, it was my misfortune to attend to thofe who advifed me to have the ivy cut off for the good of the tree; from that moment it seemed to decay, and the fecond year fcarcely put out a leaf; I do not recollect its dimenfions, but I know that one length of its ftem fold at 1s. 6d. per foot,

for

for 5l. 12s. for the purpofe of making bellows for furnace, and the remainder brought the whole value to about 10l. This, though certainly a confiderable produce for an afh tree, we fhall find hereafter greatly exceeded by the fale of fome others in the neighbourhood of Dublin.

Near the bridge of *Rathdrum* is a moft picturefque *Sycamore* above 11 feet round, and at two miles from that town on the road to Shillela, there was lately belonging to Thomas King, Efq; a ftill greater tree of that fpecies, being 15 feet in circumference, with the moft beautiful head in proportion; this was the largeft fycamore I ever faw; the beft now in the county is at *Weftafton*, the feat of Thomas Acton, Efq; where in general the trees are of very confiderable magnitude.

Dunganftown the eftate of William Hoey, Efq; contains feveral very fine trees of different fpecies; but an old avenue of *Spanifh chefnuts* which ftood in the domain 'till this fummer 1793 for 110 *years*, contained amongft them fome of the fineft fpecimens of that charming tree, which

I ever met with—they are now no more—but I must do Mr. Hoey the juſtice to ſay, that he withheld his conſent to their being felled, till they exhibited ſuch ſymptoms of decay as rendered them no longer *ornamental*. I took a laſt view of them as they lay on the ground, after all their branches had been lopped off and carried away; from their ſize, form, and greyiſh colour, they ſtrongly reminded me of the deſcription given by travellers, of huge *crocodiles* ſunning themſelves on the banks of the Nile. I meaſured the three firſt I came to, one was 16 feet 6 inches round, another 15 feet, and the third 14 feet 3 inches; the length of one 36 feet, and of another 24, and 12 feet round at the *ſmalleſt end*.

Having viewed theſe remains for the laſt time, with *great regret*, I had the pleaſure of finding an admired line of *Yew trees* in full vigour, as remarkable for their *form* as the cheſnuts had been for their *ſize*, this conſiſts of about 30 trees, moſt of them 6 feet round, perfectly ſtraight and ſmooth in the ſtem as a young aſh tree, for about 7 feet 6 inches from the ground; where they begin

begin to throw out branches, and thence continue a rich close mass of green foliage for full 25 feet above their clear stems, resembling a considerable superstructure raised over a regular colonade---had such a growth of *yew* been common in this kingdom in the days of archery, we should not have wanted acts of parliament requiring the importation of *yew bow-staves* from *Spain*.

Every species of myrtle seemed formerly almost indigenous at *Dunganstown*; I have known the narrow leaved Italian in full flower there, above 16 feet high:---Of two old stems I measured last summer, one was 17 inches round, the other was within one inch of two feet, or eight inches diameter. The most promising tree now here is an *Ash*, 12 feet round with a straight stem, and quite clear of branches for 30 feet, where it measures 10 feet round, and the arms extend in beautiful forms 28 yards.

At *Rossana* the seat of Mrs. Tighe, and on the estate adjoining, we have several specimens of fine timber; amongst these the *Milltown oak* is moſt conſiderable; till very lately the head had ſcarcely loſt a ſingle branch, and formed a huge canopy of 36 yards extent over a clear ſtem 19 feet round, and 9 feet high: yet notwithſtanding theſe very great dimenſions, I have good reaſon for being of opinion, that this tree has not grown from an acorn *without tranſplantation*; from ſeveral circumſtances it appears to have been once a *breaſt-quick* in the face of a ditch.

At *Mountuſher* there are ſome great evergreen oak, from 6 to 8 feet round, the wood of which is hard beyond conception and ſeems incapable of decay; but the *Silver fir* next the houſe are particularly deſerving of our notice, as the largeſt trees of their ſpecies I have ever ſeen; one meaſuring 12 feet round, the other 11 feet 6, upwards of 100 feet high, and carrying nearly the ſame girths for 36 feet.

Conſiderable as the magnitude of ſome of the above foreſt trees muſt be allowed to be, we know they are *exceeded* by ſeveral of the ſame kind

kind in England*; but the following dimensions of a fruit tree, and a flowering-shrub both now standing in the county of *Wicklow* have scarcely been any where equalled;

unless

---

* I have selected out of many others the following instances of extraordinary size and great value of some oaks now standing in England, as likely to be acceptable to such of my Readers as may not have had an opportunity of viewing the trees, or perusing the works from which the following particulars are extracted:

The SWILCAR OAK in *Needwood Forest*,

Measures 21 feet in circumference at 5 feet from the ground.

Sir WALTER BAGOT's WALKING-STICK,

Measures 16 feet round at 6 feet from the ground, 35 feet of clear stem, then 40 feet of branches and a clear stem over that for a considerable height, valued at 60l.

Duke of PORTLAND's WALKING-STICK, at *Welbeck*,

Circumference at bottom 21 feet, at a yard from the ground 14 feet, 111 feet high, contents 440 feet of timber.

The

unless we admit the chesnut *di centi cavalli* on Mount *Ætna* to be produced as one of the *former* class. The fruit tree I allude to, is a
cherry

The Duke's Porters at *Welbeck*.

Circumference of one at bottom 38 feet, at a yard high 27 feet, height 98 feet, contents 840 feet: circumference of the other at bottom 34 feet, at a yard high 23 feet, 88 feet in height, contents 744 feet.

Parliament Oak in *Clipston-park*,

Measures 28 feet 6 inches at a yard from the ground.

Birchland Oak in *Sherwood Forest*,

Measures 27 feet 4 inches round in the *smallest* part.

Middleton Oak,

Measures 20 feet round at 3 feet—25 feet clear stem, then several tire of branches, over that a clear stem of 15 feet which makes the whole stem 65 feet—50l. has been long since refused for this tree.

Shire Oak in Earl Fitzwilliam's Park at *Wentworth*,

Height of the stem 50 feet, by what dimensions in circumference I cannot exactly state, but there is 306 solid *cherry* at the Rev. Mr. Truel's at *Clonmannin*; which measures 15 feet round the stem at 5 from the ground, it is in perfect health and full

---

lid feet, in 25 feet of the grosseft part, which is valued to 61l. 5s. 0d.—value of the whole tree 111l. 15s.

Holt Forest Oak near *Bentley*,

Measures 34 feet in circumference at 7 feet high.

Lord Petre's Chesnut at *Writtle* in *Essex*,

Measures 46 feet one inch round at 5 feet high, or full 15 feet diameter.

Lord Ducie's Chesnut at *Totworth* in *Gloucestershire*,

Measures 46 feet 6 inches in circumference at 6 feet from the ground.—This tree is supposed to be 1100 years old, having been called the *Great Chesnut* in the reign of King John.

The Cowthorpe Oak near *Wetherby*,

In circumference close to the ground 78 *feet*, at 3 feet from the ground 48, its height in the shattered state it is now in, 85 feet, its principal limb extends 16 *yards* from the trunk—for further particulars of this truly wonderful tree, I refer the reader to the last edition of Evelyn's Sylva, by Mr. Hunter, where he will find a sketch &c. of it made on the spot by my ingenious and amiable friend *William Burgh*, of York, Esq;

full bearing, the fruit very finely flavoured, of the *Upton-mazard* kind.

The shrub which I hold to be the most singular in this or in any other kingdom is the celebrated arbutus at *Mount-Kennedy*, the charming seat of our present Commander in Chief, already noticed by Mr. Fortescue in his hints on planting, and by Mr. Young in his tour through Ireland. The stem below its first division as measured by Mr. Fortescue in 1773, was 13 feet 9 inches round, it had been planted in a small garden enclosed with high walls at a period previous to the present century; as the castle was destroyed towards the end of the last, this ascertains its age to exceed *one hundred years*.

General Cuninghame in dressing his domain found it necessary to take away the walls and level the ground of the old castle garden, which exposed the arbutus to storm on that side where it had been sheltered for so many years, and where from its situation near the wall no great

roots

roots had been formed, the confequence was, that in a high wind about twenty-two years ago the root was torn up, the trunk fplit in two, one half nearly buried in the ground, and the other forced into a very oblique pofition, greatly mutilated indeed, but ftill thro' fkilful management very beautiful; frefh healthy fhoots having fprung up from the branches, where they have been inferted in the ground in the manner of *layers*, and fome young plants introduced amongft them, fo as in the whole to make one of the moft pleafing groupes or maffes of this charming fpecies of evergreen, which is any where to be met with. I meafured it on Chriftmas-day 1793; the principal ftem now ftanding, which, as I faid before, is but barely half the tree, is 8 feet in circumference, this divides into four branches, one of which is 4 feet 10 inches, and the fmalleft 3 feet round; a branch which was fawed off at 9 feet from the trunk, meafures 2 feet 9 inches at the fmall end; the whole was then in full beauty of foliage berry and bloffom *at once.*

I have often visited this extraordinary tree, for who has ever been *once* at *Mount-Kennedy*, that did not wish to go *again*, and I never viewed it but with *encreased wonder* and *delight*.

Tiny-Park, the seat of Sir Skeffington Smyth, Bart. affords many objects well worth the attention of the arborist; we here find an *Ash* in a very exposed situation, on the bank of a ditch evidently growing from a transplanted tree, and that once *cut down*, the circumference of which in the *smallest* part of the trunk somewhat exceeds 19 feet, or 6 feet 4 inches diameter.— There is another near the old house which has been very beautiful, but is now much decayed; it measures 13 feet round, and carries that size with a straight clear stem for about 25 feet.— A third on the top of a dry bank overpowered with ivy, is 18 feet in circumference; there are three noble *Beech* together, the smallest 14 feet round, the next 15 feet 6 inches at the butt, and 14 feet 8 inches at 7 feet from the ground; the third, which is one of the most beautiful and fairest trees imaginable, is 16 feet 3 inches round, and continues nearly of that girth for
36 *feet*

36 *feet high.* There are many Portugal laurel from 4 to 5 feet round, and abundance of common laurel above 6 feet in circumference; some with clear stems for 16 feet high. I measured one of 7 feet round or 2 feet 4 inches diameter whose stem and branches together were above 36 feet in height. There is a *Scots-fir* of 10 feet round whose bulk is continued for 25 feet, a spruce fir 8 feet in circumference and of the same girth for 20 feet, and considerable timber for 50 feet more, and another 9 feet round, of very great height, yet the head perfect and beautiful, with all its branches weeping, which in spruce-fir is a mark of luxuriant health.

At *Ballygannon*, the seat of J. P. Scot, Esq; is a variegated silver holly remarkably beautiful from the richness and closeness of its head, the stem is about five feet round, and the whole 28 feet high.

There is a fine specimen of the *Pinus Sativa* or *true Stone Pine* at *Old-court*, the seat of John Edwards, Esq. the stem is very gross, straight, and free from knots for a considerable heighth,

with

with a great branching head; it grows near an old caftle, and gives the fcene an appearance of what we may find in fome of the landfcapes of Pouffin and Claude Loraine

At *Kilruddery* the antient feat of the Earls of Meath, are feveral very large evergreens of various kinds and of great beauty; the *Ilex* in particular, grows here as well as in any part of Italy.

In Lord Powerfcourt's romantic park which contains the celebrated waterfall, the growth of the old *Oak* adds much to the picturefque fcenery; he has alfo fome fine trees nearer *Powerfcourt*: I meafured one *Afh* with a clear ftem of 20 feet in height, which was 15 feet in circumference.

Having now finifhed the furvey I propofed of the maritime fide of the county of Wicklow, I fhall prefent the reader with the refult of my enquiries in the county of Dublin; and firft,

At

At *Old Connaught* near Bray, there are some *Bay traes* of extraordinary size, several of them 8 feet in circumference, and till last year there was one whose stem exceeded 11 feet in girth or 3 feet 8 inches diameter.

At *Loughlinstown* there is an old *Elm* of great size and formerly of considerable beauty, and well placed on a high knowl, but in dressing the ground some time since, the roots have been in-injured, and all the branches have decayed in consequence. There are some very large ash in the Earl of Ely's park at *Rathfarnham*, but by far the finest trees in the neighbourhood of Dublin are at *Luttrelstown* the seat of the Earl of Car-hampton, whose good taste in rural decoration has done justice to the many natural beauties it possesses; I have scarcely any where met with so many trees of different kinds which have attain-ed to such great bulk as here — in 1793 I mea-sured a *Scots-fir* eighty-five years growth from the seed, of 11 feet 6 inches in circumference, and another of very great height 11 feet 10 inches round or 4 feet diameter, which I believe

exceeeds

exceeds the dimensions of the largest foreign deal ever imported into this kingdom; these stand amongst oak and other trees on very high ground though flat at top for a considerable extent, and must when young have been greatly exposed to storm; several *Ash* in a valley measured from 11 to 13 feet 6 inches round, and were of an extraordinary height; one of these sold since I measured it for 13l. some time before an *Elm* beginning to decay was sold for 16l.; but the celebrated *Elm* by the road side is still in perfect health and beauty, measuring fairly 18 feet 10 inches round the butt, and 14 feet 4 inches at 8 feet from the ground, and is very gross timber for 40 feet more.

Before I quit *Luttrelstown* I must mention a circumstance which I do not recollect to have noticed elsewhere, viz. a vigorous growth of young *Sycamore* from the keys of different ages and size, up to 20 feet high or more amidst *old Scots-fir*, and in a great measure *under their drip*; this may give a hint for the embellishment of Scots-fir groves, which are in general a most
disagreeable

disagreeable object when they begin to decay, and have been hitherto confidered as almoft incapable at that time of fupporting any other tree.

At *Leixlip Caftle*, the eftate of the Right Honourable Thomas Conolly, there is a row of *Afh* trees, 18 in number, which deferve attention for their uniform great growth, on a very bleak expofure, they meafure from 9 to 12 feet round, with fair ftems of confiderable heighth, and fine branching heads.

Not far from hence at *St. Wolftans*, in the county of Kildare, the late charming refidence of the learned and ingenious Bifhop of Killaloe, to whofe obliging communication I am indebted for the following particulars, ftood an *Elm* which till the year 1762, was perhaps the fineft tree of its fpecies in the world; the diameter of the head taken from the extremities of the lower branches exceeded 34 *yards*; but in the autumn of that year the two principal arms fell from the trunk in one night, apparently from their own weight.

weight, as the weather was perfectly calm; the timber contained in these branches alone sold for 5 *guineas*; in this situation the tree continued till the winter of 1776, when a violent storm tore up the whole by the roots with a great mass of soil and rock adhering to them. Some time previous to this the trunk had been carefully measured and was found to be 38 feet 6 inches in circumference; it had been hollow for some time, and the value of its timber by no means answered what might have been expected from the sale of the two branches in 1762; we have nothing certain as to its age, but tradition supposes it to have been planted by the Monks of *St. Wolstan*, some time before the dissolution of that monastery which happened in the year 1538.

After regretting the fall of this colossal tree, the reader will learn with pleasure, that not far from St. Wolstans, at *Carton*, the magnificent domain of the Duke of Leinster, through whose polite attention I was favoured with the measurement, there now stands in full health an *Elm* 14 feet 8 inches round near the bottom, or 4 feet 10

inches

inches diameter, and thence gradually diminishing like the shaft of a doric column, being 13 feet in circumference, or 4 feet 4 inches diameter at 16 feet from the ground, and containing in the whole 169 solid feet of timber, with a fine head and in great vigour.

Very different from the perfect state of this beautiful *Elm* is that of the old *Ash* of Donirey near Clare-castle in the county of Galway, as communicated to me by Mr. Hardy, (inspector of claims for premiums offered by the Dublin Society) who is himself a very skilful arborist, and from whose great fidelity in his reports, the following dimensions may with certainty be relied on: at 4 *feet* from the ground it measures 14 *yards* or 42 *feet* in circumference, which is 14 *feet* diameter; at 6 *feet* high, 33 *feet* round, or 11 *feet* diameter: these dimensions nearly equal the celebrated *Cowthorpe oak*, but the trunk has long been quite hollow, a little school having been kept in it about 25 years ago; there are but few branches remaining, but these are fresh and very vigorous.

I feel much indebted to the Earl of Defart for the trouble he was fo obliging to take in procuring me the following meafurement of fome of the very fine trees which ornament his antient feat in the county of Kilkenny.

I have felected a few only of each kind out of a lift containing many more of nearly equal fize, viz:

Six *Oak* from 12 feet to 16 feet 3 inches in circumference.

Six *Afh* from 11 feet 3 inches to 13 feet 4 inches in ditto.

Six *Elm* from 9 feet 6 inches to 10 feet 8 inches, ditto.

Six *Beech* from 11 feet to 12 feet round; thefe no doubt are fine trees, but what I think more remarkable, are

Six *Spruce-fir* from 9 feet 6 inches to 10 feet 6 inches in circumference. I had often heard thefe *fir* mentioned as the fineft trees of their fpecies in the kingdom, and was happy to find
that

that they are still in being. There are few soils in which the *spruce-fir* will attain the above size; in general they decay at a much earlier period, nor is this tree inclined to grossness of stem so much as the *Silver* and *Scots-fir* in proportion to its height. The same may be said of the *Larch*, I have seen some of great age and prodigious height in the Alps, but never of extraordinary bulk; we shall find this difference in our own plantations, even where the *Larch* grows with the greatest rapidity in the beginning; amongst other instances which I am acquainted with, I find at Charles Bury's, Esq; at *Charleville* in the King's county, where there are abundance of fine *Larch*, that few exceed 6 feet 6 inches round, whilst the *Silver-fir* of nearly the same standing, measure from 8 to 10 feet in circumference.

Near *Kennity Church* in the King's county is an *Ash* celebrated for its great dimensions and for certain religious ceremonies which have for many years been observed with respect to this tree, close to which the lower class of people when passing by with a funeral, lay the corpse

down

down for a few minutes, fay a prayer, and then throw a ftone to encreafe the number, which have been accumulating for years round the root; its circumference is 21 feet 10 inches, or 7 feet 3 inches in diameter, the trunk 17 feet high before the branches break out, which are of great bulk, fome of them as grofs as the body of a horfe: For the above particular account I am obliged to Thomas Bernard, Efq; of *Caftletown*, on a part of which this extraordinary tree is fituated.

We have another fpecimen of the great growth of *Afh* at *Kilmurry* the glebe of the Rev. Mr. Huleat near Rofcrea, who was fo obliging to have it meafured at my defire; round the butt near the ground it is 27 feet, at 3 feet higher 25 feet in circumference; the height of the trunk is about 13 feet, but the branches very much decayed.

If the magnitude of feveral of the individual trees before-mentioned appears to the reader in that light in which in truth it ought to do, confidering

fidering the many chances there are againſt a tree ever attaining it, from the great length of time neceſſary, and the various accidents to which it is expoſed during its early growth, and ſtill more from *avarice* and caprice at a more advanced age; his admiration will greatly encreaſe, when he is informed, that their ſeveral dimenſions are nearly equal'd by thoſe of eighteen trees in *one demeſne*, which is the fact at *Curraghmore* the princely ſeat of the Marquis of Waterford, from whom I have had the honour of receiving the following particulars of meaſurement accurately taken at my requeſt in the courſe of this April 1794:

(142)

SIX ASH.

Height of clear ftem.	Round the butt.	Round the top of the trunk, at the height before meafured.
Feet. In.	Feet. In.	Feet. In.
No. 1—17	16 - 6	9
2—14	18 - 9	16 - 6
3—15	22 - 6	20 - 4
4—15	23	18
5—13	24 - 6	20 - 3
6—13 9	33 - 9	22 - 6

SIX BEECH.

Height of clear ftem.	Round the butt.	Round the top of the ftem.
Feet. In.	Feet. In.	Feet. In.
No. 1—18	12	6
2—14	12 - 10	8
3—15	13	7 - 6
4—14	13	8
5—20	13 - 6	6
6—14	16 - 6	14

SIX OAK.

Height of clear ftem.	Round the butt.	Round the top of the ftem.
Feet. In.	Feet. In.	Feet. In.
No. 1—21 - 6	14 - 4	11 - 5
2—27	15 - 4	11 - 5
3—23	17	10
4—23 - 9	17 - 6	10 - 4
5—23 - 6	17 - 6	10 - 6
6—25	21 - 9	12

When

When to the above we might add above 200 more trees in the fame demefne, which meafure from 10 to 14 feet round, we muft allow that *Curragh-more* is as unrivall'd in this, as in feveral other circumftances of magnificence and beauty.

I have the pleafure to find that the celebrated *Holly* in *Ennisfallen-ifland* in the *Lake of Killarney*, mentioned by Mr. Fortefcue, is ftill in perfect health and vigour; it was meafured this prefent year by William Caldbeck, Efq; in company with Chief Baron Yelverton, and proves to be nearly 15 feet in circumference, the ftem about the fame height, and the branches very confiderable.

From feveral inftances which have fallen within my knowledge, I might fairly affert that the longevity of certain fpecies of *Evergreens*, and the great magnitude to which they arrive is in direct proportion to the *flownefs* of their growth. I have never feen any of the Fir or Pine tribe, all allow'd to be quick growers, ever equal to the above *Holly* in dimenfions, which though of very flow growth muft yield on the other hand in point of fize to a tree of ftill flower, viz. the *Yew*; many of which I have feen in England full as large again as the above *Holly*.

We had feveral fine fpecimens of this tree formerly in Ireland—in the mountainous parts of the county of *Wicklow* it was certainly *indigenous*, and ftill grows in a few fpots which are luckily inacceffable to mifchievous cattle, and avaricious land-owners—there was within thefe fifty years a fingle *Yew-tree* adjoining one of the feven churches in *Glandalough*, from whofe lofty trunk, about 16 feet round, extended on every fide a mafs of clofe branches, which fhaded from the fun, and fheltered from every inclemency of weather, the picturefque ruin it adorned, and *all* the church-yard. This I have had from the indubitable authority of feveral who ftill well remember it, when in its full beauty, on a hot fummer's day, at a time that numbers were regaling themfelves under its fhade, a gentleman of the party, who pleaded the authority of an agent to the See, (but whofe employer I am perfuaded could not have ever viewed the fcene),

had

had all its principal limbs and branches fawed off clofe to the trunk, for the *value of the timber*—from that time to the prefent, which may be about forty years, the poor remains have been in a conftant ftate of decay; it has fcarcely put out a branch, the bark has fallen off, and a large *Holly* is growing up through the fiffures of the ftem; fo that I confider it too far gone to enumerate it amongft the large trees ftill ftanding in the county of Wicklow.

We may fee a fine *Yew* which has met with a better fate at *Fornace*, the feat of Richard Neville, Efq; in the county of Kildare; the ftem, which is very clear for this fpecies of tree, meafures 12 feet round at 6 feet high; the branches extend 66 feet, and add much to a pleafing fequeftered fcene near an old ruin, amidft *Holly* and *Laurel* of extraordinary bulk and great height.

At the Earl of Courtown's admired retreat in the county of Wexford, there is a very fine *Afh* which in point of beauty would now have equall'd any in the kingdom if a part of its

great

great head had not been cut away to prevent injury to the dwelling-houfe, clofe to which it ftands; it is 15 feet 2 inches round and carries nearly that fize for 13 feet in height; the main branches are very grofs for 26 feet from the bole, and beyond that there is ftill a confiderable length and great quantity of faleable timber; it is fuppofed to have attained this bulk within 90 years, and it is a circumftance well deferving the planter's notice, that during a great part of that period this tree muft have been expofed to violent blafts from the *fea*; but here I cannot help obferving, that amongft other uncommon charms, *Courtown* poffeffes *one* in a very fuperior degree, viz. that of a vigorous growth of timber almoft to the water's edge on the *fea fhore*: fo that within a few yards of a fequeftered inland fcene, where a clear ftream winds beautifully through a wooded valley, you may take fhipping to any part of the world; nor need you wait long for an opportunity, particular circumftances of anchorage, &c. inducing moft veffels in their paffage along this coaft, to caft anchor for

fome

some time in that spot which terminates a visto from one of the drawing-room windows.

I have long observed the *Ash* to be capable of arriving to the utmost perfection, in a greater variety of soils, and bearing a more severe exposure than any other tree ; I do not recollect this quality to have been taken notice of by any arborist amongst the many excellent ones it may with justice lay claim to, if we except *Spencer's* negative compliment in the *Fairy Queen*, viz.—

" *The ash for nothing ill*———."

which certainly would imply a great deal, if we had reason to think he had any thing farther in contemplation than the excellence of the *timber*. I have described the *Ash* at *Avondale* growing to 14 feet in circumference, or above 4½ feet in diameter in the edge of the *river* ; that at *Courtown* is within the influence of the *sea*, whilst those I shall now mention at *Arles church* in the *Queen's county* are growing in a *dry* soil, on a high knowl or sort of *Barrow* open on every side to the *storm* blowing over a long tract of flat country;

try; nor could they from their first planting have ever enjoyed the *least shelter*; add to this that they are elevated on the top of a steep bank in a single row round the church yard, and were in all probability planted of such a size as to be at once out of the reach of cattle, notwithstanding all these circumstances against them they are very fine trees; of *two* I measured, one was 10 feet round in the smallest part of the bole, the other 11 feet 6 inches at 6 feet from the ground, but these (as has been said of the other trees of England in comparison with the *Cowthorpe Oak*) are but mere *children of the forest* when compared with the *ash* of *Leix* in the same county. This celebrated piece of antiquity stands on the high road between Monasterevan and Port-Arlington, and though it has long ceased to have any pretensions to *beauty*, is still one of the most *picturesque* and *magnificent* objects of the kind I have ever met with; I measured it in April 1792; at one foot from the ground it was 40 *feet 6 inches* round, and at 5 feet higher which is actually the *smallest* part of the trunk it is full 25 feet in circumference or 8 *feet 4 inches diameter*;

this

this massive stem is full 9 feet high, but the enormous grossness of the branches at their springing from the bole, and the *horizontal* position which most of them immediately take, make the stem appear much *shorter* than it really is.

At some paces from this venerable antient, whose branches though much mutilated, extend full 70 feet, stands the *small* tree of *Leix*, as it is called, though it is 14 feet 4 inches round in the *smallest* part you can measure, it grows on the top of a dry bank, part of the fence of a church-yard, in a situation I should hardly have thought favourable to that rapid growth which its appearance indicates; it is by no means an *old* tree, and if suffered to remain, may in procefs of time even exceed the bulk of its present companion. The lover of trees will hear with pleasure, that it is in no danger of falling at this time, being on the estate of the *Earl of Port-Arlington*, an excellent arborist and one of the most extensive planters and improvers in the kingdom :— On viewing the works which have lately been carried on in his demesne of *Emo-Park*, and a

very

very great houfe now building, I was at a lofs which to admire moft. the extent and boldnefs of defign, or the pleafing effect refulting from the tafte and judgment with which it is carried into execution.

There are feveral *Scots-fir* here from 8 to 9 feet in circumference, ftanding fingle with clear ftems from 20 to 30 feet high, and large wild branching heads, but richly clothed with leaves; in this ftate the *Scots-fir* or *Pine* becomes a very *picturefque* tree, and in fome fituations highly ornamental. There are alfo feveral fine *Beech*, *Elm* and *Lime*, and a handfome *Yew-tree*, with a good head and clear ftem 8 feet round; but the lovers of coppices and planting, will be ftill better pleafed to find fome acres of hop-ground, part of which has borne fine crops for many years, and what has been lately planted promifes as well as poffible for the time. The growth of *hops* and attention to trees go hand in hand, thefe two fpecies of improvement mutually affift each other, and Lord Port-Arlington has found his hops to be profitable beyond expectation.

At

At *Rathleague*, the feat of Sir John Parnell, Bart. though the traveller's attention is naturally attracted by a beautiful piece of water, decorated with extenfive plantation, and a handfome doric Temple on its banks—he may find in the more fequeftered part of the demefne, fome very confiderable trees; there are many *Beech* from 9 to 7 feet round with ftraight clear ftems, of extraordinary height; and feveral very fine *Oak*, amongft which I meafured one of 9 feet round, as growing in my opinion from a tranfplanted tree which had been headed clofe down at the time of tranfplanting; there are alfo very large *Wyche-Elm*, and *Afh* : But Lord Afhbrook at *Caftledurrow* poffeffes an *Afh* which I think on the whole is the moft ornamental tree of its fpecies that has ever fallen within my obfervation — it meafured in October 1793, 18 feet in circumference or 6 feet in diameter, and carried nearly the fame dimenfions for 14 feet, the branches extending 45 feet from the ftem in almoft *every* direction, and would in *all*, but from part being fhortened on one fide in favour of an out office unfortunately built too near this beautiful tree,

which

which in fact deserved to have every circumstance in its vicinity considered as a *secondary* object.

I have often observed that the growth of white-thorn in *Ireland* far exceeds any I have ever met with on the other side of the water; there are in this neighbourhood at Robert Stubber's, Esq; at *Moyne*, several white-thorn of 7 and 8 feet circumference with heads finely formed, and great in proportion, so that when in flower there can be nothing more beautiful; I measured one 5 feet 4 inches round the stem at 9 feet high, the branches extending thirteen yards. Another 7 feet 6 inches round the stem in the *smallest* part, the head entire, and covering a circle of 36 feet diameter, and a third whose branches extended round a very fair stem 24 feet on every side; this last is one of the most beautiful thorns I ever saw; but the largest I recollect to have ever seen, is at Lord Gormanstown's in the county of Meath; it was about 10 feet in circumference several years since, it stood in the high road, and had received some injury and

was

was hooped round with bands of iron when I laſt ſaw it, ſo that peihaps it may have ſince decayed.

Sir Robert Staples's demeſne at *Dunmore*, amongſt other pleaſing circumſtances, poſſeſſes ſome fine old oak, many of them 12 feet round from old ſtools: the banks of the *Nore* in general afford a good growth of timber for ſome miles adjoining; but the fineſt trees by far are at *Abbeleix* the ſeat of Lord Viſcount De Veſci; we may here find an *Oak* of 20 feet 6 inches in circumference, or nearly 7 feet *diameter* at a foot from the ground, and 16 feet 9 inches round at 5 feet 3 inches high, and a horſe cheſnut whoſe rich foilage forms a ſpreading canopy over a circle of 72 feet *diameter*.

With theſe two beautiful ſpecimens of great perfection in their kinds, not unworthy of the charming·place*, in which they are ſituated, I

ſhall

---

* The growth of timber in general at *Abbeleix*, is equal to ſome of the beſt wooded demeſnes in England, and no where

shall for the present close my detail, which I fear has been already *too circumstantial* for the generality of readers, and on the other hand, not sufficiently

---

where is the *useful* and *agreeable* more intimately blended, than on the surrounding estate. Amongst many other pleasing circumstances, we are often reminded of that selected as an object of delight by Milton in his Allegro:—

> " *Hard by a Cottage chimney smoaks,*
> " *From betwixt two aged Oaks.*"

The education and useful employment of the infant poor, is *here*, as at *Rossana* and *Bellevie*, in the county of *Wicklow*, interwoven with the morning amusements of the place, whilst the comfortable, and at the same time *picturesque* cottages, with their accompanyment of eglantine and honey-suckle in the little-paled in gardens, at once *decorate* the scene, and afford *real comfort* to a happy tenantry.

To the honor indeed of the present age, the amusements and studies of several of the first rank in this, as well as our sister kingdom, are such, as conduce at once to the ornament and improvement of their respective countries. Our amiable Sovereign is not only an extensive planter, but amongst other branches of useful information, which he is eminently possessed of, is considered as one of the most scientific botanists in Europe.

ficiently *full* in the eyes of those who may perhaps justly think that they are acquainted with trees which deserve to be noticed *as well* at least, if not *better* than some which I have described: to the first I must observe, that in thus particularizing such remarkable trees as fell within my observation, I have only followed the example of the much approved of and ingenious author of the *Sylva*: I have attempted (though at a great distance I confess indeed in *every respect*) to do at this time in Ireland, what Mr. *Evelyn* did in England at the close of the last century, from an opinion, that nothing would *more* conduce to the advancement of those objects for which he had

undertaken

The first nobility, and highest in office in England, pride themselves on the character of *good Agriculturists*, and *spirited improvers*; several of the same class with us furnish examples equally *worthy of imitation*. The Duke of Leinster, Marquisses of Waterford, Downshire, and Abercorn, Earls of Shannon, Charlemont, and Port-Arlington; Lord De Vesci, Lord Mountjoy, the Speaker, Chancellor of the Exchequer, the late Teller Mr. Conyngham, and our present Commander in Chief, afford, amongst very many others, the strongest proof of the truth of this assertion.

undertaken his work, viz. the *encouragement* of *planting*, and *preservation of woods*, for the supply of *timber for the navy*.

Exclusive of a natural inclination to follow such very respectable authority, I had another inducement for registering the measurement of a considerable number of trees, which was the consideration, that by so doing alone, the growth they may make within a certain period, can possibly be *ascertained*, in order to resolve that very material question in rural œconomics, and very intimately interwoven with my subject, viz.— whether after a given time, it is adviseable to suffer a timber-tree to *stand*, where *profit alone* is the object? we have already seen that an *Oak* is in a state of encreasing value, almost in geometrical progression from forty to eighty years growth : what I have done, may in a few years hence by having fresh measurements taken, very well ascertain how long *after* that period its value continues to *encrease*. These considerations, I hope, will excuse me to such as might otherwise think I had dwelt too long on a matter of

mere

mere curiofity.—To thofe who may fuppofe that I have defpifed their groves, and flighted their favourite dryads, I flatter myfelf I need fay no more to obtain a better opinion of me, than barely to affure them, that *want of time*, and in confequence a want of fufficient materials, has been the fole caufe of this apparent neglect; and that if I fhall at any time hereafter, be favoured with fuch information as may enable me to do juftice to thofe fpecimens of fine timber now ftanding, which have not already fallen within my notice, I fhall take another opportunity of making a proper ufe of it, and will thankfully acknowledge the obligation.

ON THE RAPID
GROWTH OF TREES IN PARTICULAR SITUATIONS.

As the foregoing examples of extraordinary magnitude and value of trees after a certain age, were intended for the confideration of the *wood-owner*, as evident proofs of the advantage refulting from the *prefervation of timber* to a proper age, and of leaving a fufficient number of *referves* at every fall; the following inftances of the extraordinary quick growth of feveral trees of different fpecies, are felected out of very many others, as moft likely to encourage the exertions of the *Planter*, by giving him an affurance of enjoying within a reafonable period, the fruits of his labour.

One of the moft remarkable which I have been made acquainted with, was an *Oak* at *Cahirnane*, near the celebrated Lake of Killarney, the feat of R. T. Herbert, Efq; which, in the year 1739 would have been cut for the purpofe of twifting into the back-band of a cart, but from the carter's taking notice of its fuperior height and

and beauty, to feveral others of the fame age at that time furrounding it, none of which could have exceeded eight years from the acorn.—In the year 1785 fome mifchievous perfon ftripped off the bark nearly all round the ftem: Mr. Herbert confidered the tree as irrecoverably loft, but it was fo beautiful at the time, that he fuffered it to ftand for another year; it was then felled, when the bark produced little fhort of *three pounds*, and the timber was valued to as much more, fo that the tree in its fifty-fixth year was worth 6*l.*; which is full double to what I have eftimated a tree of that age in any preceding calculation.—It is worth obferving, that the timber proved hard and folid like that of a tree which had continued a confiderable time at a ftand, though it was in fuch vigour, and fine ftate of growing the year before it was felled; this is only to be accounted for from the fap having ceafed to flow freely, from the time when the bark was ftripped off; a circumftance much in favour of Monf. du Hamel's directions in his treatife "*Des Arbres et Arbuftes*," where he advifes ftripping the bark off all trees as they ftand, stand, the year previous to their fall—the superior goodness which I have always remarked in the timber of such *Fir-trees* of different species as have appeared somewhat decayed at top, or *rampiked* before they were felled, is another proof in favour of Monf. du Hamel's method; but, as on the other hand I have heard it observed that no considerable growth has ever been made from the old stools of *Oak* managed in this way: I should not indeed without more experience, recommend the practice to any extent, in such woods as we wish to preserve for future coppices. From *theory* it is natural to suppose, that a tree felled when all its sap had gone down, and was concenter'd as is the general opinion in its *root*, would be the most likely to throw up a vigorous shoot; but from long observation I can aver that the root of an *Oak* never produces a finer growth of young wood, than when the tree is felled about the first week in *June*, in full leaf and vigour, and at the moment when the sap is most abundant in the stem and branches.—The same may be observed of the *White-thorn*; I have known many roots decay

or

or throw out only a few weakly fhoots when cut at that feafon when all the *fap was down* ; and it gives me great pleafure to be confirmed in the truth of this obfervation, by fome of the moft ingenious writers on fubjects of rural œconomy of the prefent day*.

In addition to the above inftance of an *Oak's* early arriving to confiderable value, Mr. Herbert has given me the following meafurement of fix *Oak* taken indifcriminately (except the laft,) out of very many more of the fame fize, growing on his demefne from acorns fown in the year 1760—they were meafured in this year 1794, at 5 feet from the ground, being in their thirty-fourth year.

No.	Feet.	In.
1	3	0
2	3	2
3	3	$2\frac{1}{2}$
4	3	7
5	3	8
6	4	11

---

* Vide Marfhall's Minutes of Agriculture and Planting in the midland fhires of England. Min. 146.

He favoured me at the same time with the measurement of six *Wyche* or native *Irish Elm*, produced by layers from the stool of a tree felled for that purpose in 1766, consequently about 26 years growth at the very most.

No.	Feet.	In.
1	3	11
2	4	0
3	4	2
4	4	5
5	4	9

at five feet from the ground.

6 — 5 — 1 at 3 feet where it forked, and produced 2 branches each 3 feet 2 inches round;—though these also (except the last) were taken indiscriminately out of many more of the same age and dimensions, yet we find that three out of the six would cut into *twelve-inch plank* at 26 years standing from the transplanted layer.

At *Bellevüe* in the county of Galway, the seat of Walter Laurence, Esq; a great improver and extensive planter, the *Spanish Chesnuts* afford many remarkable instances of quick growth; they had been, when measured in 1790, 27 years transplanted, and were about 5 years old when removed,

removed, consequently their age did not exceed 32 years from the nut, yet many of them were then 5 feet in circumference at a foot from the ground, and 4 feet 8 inches at 6 feet from the lower measurement, which last dimension continued with little diminution for 10 feet more; so that on an average of the different measurements, they would have afforded plank of 16 feet in length and full 12 *inches broad*, and some considerably broader, as one tree was found to measure 7 feet round at a foot from the ground, or 2 feet 4 inches diameter. This fine growth is in *strong loom* over a lime-stone rock, and offers a great inducement indeed, amongst many others, in favour of planting this incomparable tree; which for beauty of foliage, great bulk, valuable quality of timber, and longevity, is second to the *Oak* alone, whilst in quickness of growth we see that in many soils, and those far from rich, it exceeds almost every other species of timber tree.

The plantations of *Carrickglass*, in the county of Longford, the seat of Sir William Gleadowe Newcomen,

Newcomen, Bart. have in general the appearance of as great vigour and *quick growth*, as any I have ever feen, confidering that in their wide extent the foil muft often vary, but the trees have been fo judicioufly adapted, that *all* are in a flourifhing ftate; if there is a difference in their growth it feems to be in favour of the *Oak*, of which their great annual fhoots and polifhed bark give evident proof—after this character of the foil of *Carrickglafs* as particularly fuited to trees, we might naturally fuppofe that it produced the *Larch*, (a part of which fawed off was fome time fince fent into the Repofitory of the Dublin Society, by Sir William, as a fpecimen of the great growth of that fpecies of tree) but *that* came from his grounds at *Killefter*, about two miles from Dublin. It is indeed well worth notice, as having arrived to the meafurement of foot 8 inches *diameter* within 19 years, whilft the *Spruce-fir*, a part of which is placed befide the piece of *Larch*, appears to have taken 25 years from the feed to attain a *diameter* of 1 foot 7 inches; but it fhould be obferved that the *Larch* has been cut quite low with a faw into a

part

part of the *root*, whilſt the *Spruce-fir* was felled firſt with an *axe*, and then a piece cut off with a *ſaw* a foot at leaſt above the ground, cloſe to which it meaſured 6 feet round ; we muſt alſo take notice that it had been tranſplanted when full *ſeven* feet high, a circumſtance which in general, gives a great check to the growth of every ſpecies of *Fir*.

This tree, which before its top was broken off by a violent ſtorm promiſed in time to be one of the moſt beautiful of its kind in the kingdom, grew at *Avondale* before-mentioned, in the county of Wicklow---it was that feminal variety of the *Spruce* which has been denominated the long-coned Corniſh *Fir* ; the cones being frequently near a foot long, it had been tranſplanted into a little lawn in a natural wood, edged on one ſide with old *Oak*, and on the other with remarkable fine Weymouth *Pine*.---Obſerving its luxuriant growth, and a tendency to *weeping* in its branches like the *Willow*, I followed a practice which I recollected to have been mentioned to me ſome years ſince by the late Mr. Shanley,

(whoſe

(whofe fkill and natural tafte in ornamental gardening had early attracted my notice;) viz. cutting away by degrees *all* the branches for about 7 feet high, and above that every *fecond tire*; by which, as the lateral fhoots encreafe in weight, they fall into the fpace formerly occupied by the branches which were immediately below them; this, in a vigorous tree, adds much to the picturefque appearance, and is doubly pleafing as connected with the idea of perfect health and luxuriant growth; fuch was the ftate of this beautiful tree at the time of the ftorm, that the lower branches which covered a confiderable fpace on every fide, nearly touched the ground at their extremities, though they grew from the ftem at the height of 7 feet. It is fomewhat remarkable, that none of the Weymouth *Pine* though as tall as the *Spruce*, and ftanding on higher ground and more expofed to the ftorm, fuffered from it in the leaft.

The lovers of planting will pardon me for this digreffion on a favourite tree, and will be pleafed to hear that the lofs has long fince been repaired,

repaired, by the fine growth of numbers of its contemporaries.

In 1793, I felled a *Scots-fir*, one of *fifty* which had been brought to the plantation from a distance of *three* miles in a *one-horse* cart, and as they were planted but 19 years, the tree I felled could not have exceeded 27 *years* at moſt from the *seed*, and I rather think it could not have been so old as 8 years at the time of tranſplanting; there was about a foot of the butt end waſted in felling and ſawing off the rough part after the axe, yet it meaſured fully 21 inches *diameter* at an average of three ſeveral meaſurements; it was ſawed into two lengths of plank, and produced twelve in all, worth at leaſt 20 *ſhillings* the dozen; the value of the remainder of the tree more than paid the expence of felling and manufacturing the boards.

Every planter will allow, that ſuch *Fir* ſhould by no means ſtand at a greater diſtance than 9 feet from each other; and the author of the treatiſe on the *Pinus Silveſtris*, would not allow them *half* ſo much, yet even at this diſtance, and

allowing

allowing two feet to each tree for the space its stem would actually occupy, we shall find that 640 such trees will stand on an Irish acre: Now, supposing them a full third *worse* than that which I have last mentioned, and to remain *three years* longer on the ground, we shall still have a produce of 426*l*. in 30 years, or upwards of 14*l. per annum* for the *Acre*. I am well aware of the fallacy of drawing general conclusions from particular instances, and will readily allow, that on a very extensive scale some parts might fail of equal success; or if not, the very *plenty so produced*, would considerably lessen the value of the *production*; but in the present general state of the kingdom with respect to *timber*, we have little to apprehend from a *redundancy* for many years to come; and in the mean time, it would be but prudent to provide against the difficulties which we are often threatened with, in procuring timber from the northern countries of Europe, even if the attempt was not supported by such evident proofs of great and almost *immediate profit.*

I find

I find that *Weymouth Pine* planted now about 23 years, from the feed-bed, meafure from 4 feet 6 inches to 3 feet, at one foot from the ground, and from 3 feet 6 inches to 2 feet 8 inches in circumference at five feet high, and are in general above 50 feet in height.—I have numbers of *Oak* tranfplanted from a *Dublin* feed-bed in May 1780, now 14 years growth, which meafure at a foot from the ground, from one foot 10 inches to one foot 6 inches in circumference, and from one foot 3 inches to one foot round, at 4 feet above the latter meafurement; but the tree, which of all others promifes to make the greateft progrefs on the generality of our high grounds, is the *Beech;* feveral at *Avondale,* which were tranfplanted within 30 years on a fwelling ground, at that time much expofed to ftorm, are now from 7 feet 6 inches, to 6 feet 6 inches at a foot from the ground, and continue nearly of that fize from 8 to 20 feet in height: of two which were planted in a richer foil near the river, and are now juft fifty-four years old from the maſt, one meaſures 9 feet round, and the other 9 feet 6 inches.

This muſt be allowed to be a very great growth in the time, and when we add to this perfection of the *Beech*, that there appears no limit to its *duration*, as there are ſome Beech trees now in England which are ſuppoſed to have exiſted before the Norman conqueſt, yet ſtill freſh and vigorous, even when the trunk has exceeded ten yards in circumference, as I recollect a tree, which I meaſured in the great park of *Windſor*, to have done; and that whilſt the maſt in our woods is the fineſt food poſſible for ſwine, the timber is daily coming more and more into uſe, as anſwering in general every purpoſe of the *Aſh*, and found for ſome to be ſuperior; being now uſed as we are informed in thoſe very ſatisfactory letters of Thomas South, of Baſſington, Eſq. to the *Bath and Weſt of England Society*, for *planking* ſuch parts of the bottoms of ſhips as are conſtantly *under water*, and for ſluices and ſhoots, &c.

in

in mill work, we shall find no tree on the whole, that will more fully answer the Planter's expectation; as uniting in itself many of those qualities, for which individually, other trees are considered valuable.—I would not wish however, to devote the whole of an enclosure to this tree, great a favourite as it is; but taking advantage of its hardy nature, and tendency to preserve its leaves during a great part of the severest winters, I would cover with it a considerable portion of my high grounds, and allot the space within the influence of this shelter, to the production of *Oak*, *Spanish Chesnut*, *Weymouth Pine*, and such other valuable trees, as we find from many instances, are not as well qualified as the former, to bear the severity of an exposed situation, particularly in the early part of their growth.

The following are the measurements of five *Oak* taken from amongst numbers of the same age and dimensions, growing from the old stools of trees felled in one of my woods, 33 years this May, 1794:

No.	Ft.	In.		Ft.	In.	
1	3	4	⎫	— 2	9	⎫
2	3	4	⎬ at 1 foot	— 3	0	⎬ at 5 feet
3	3	9	⎬ from the	— 3	4	⎬ from the
4	4	0	⎬ ground.	— 3	7	⎬ ground.
5	4	10	⎭	— 4	0	⎭

Considerable as these dimensions must appear for their age, * to those who are apt to look on coppiced

---

* I find by an accurate measurement of the *Luccomb Oak*, which a friend of mine was so good to make at my desire, within these few months, that at this time, *viz.* in its twenty-seventh year's growth, its circumference is 4 feet 6½ inches at four feet from the ground, six feet at the place of grafting, and its height 60 feet: the fairness of its growth, the verdure and long continuance of its leaves, are sufficient motives no doubt, to induce every Planter to wish for some of those beautiful trees in his demesne; but the goodness of the *timber* yet remains

coppiced woods, as little more than a collection of broomsticks, (which in the way they are usually managed, I allow, they but too much resemble,)

---

remains to be *proved*, and from the appearance of its *bark* I fear it too much resembles what has been generally imported from America, to answer the wishes of the manufacturer, in any comparison with the Irish or English; as I have seen *foreign bark* nearly two inches in thickness in the whole, with scarcely a quarter of an inch applicable to the purposes of *tanning*.

This should make us cautious of introducing too many of the foreign varieties of Oak into such plantations as are made with a view to future profit—there are many of them indeed very beautiful; I think none more so, than the *Ragnal, Quercus Xeris* or *Turkey Oak*, whose deep indented leaves, and their particular manner of growing in groupes on the branches, have certainly a grace and richness peculiar to themselves.

This tree is no where in greater beauty than at *Collon*, in the county of Lowth, the seat of the Speaker of the House of Commons, who thro' his very extensive plantations, has found means of attracting the attention of the lovers of planting every moment, by the judicious arrangement of such an inexhaustible variety and scientific col-

femble,) I have reafon to expect, that their meafurement, at the expiration of the next five years, will ftill more exceed the ufual dimenfions of trees of the fame age; as there was not that attention paid to this wood for the firft fifteen years after the fall, which I have fince thought neceffary, and have fo ftrongly recommended in the preceding fection. † Thefe

plants

---

collection of trees and plants, as are fcarcely to be equalled unlefs in the royal gardens of *Kew*.

The *Turner* Oak has great merit in continuing in full leaf and luxuriant frefhnefs through the greater part of winter; but on the whole, we fhall find *none*, that in the end will repay the labour of either the *profitable* or *picturefque* Planter *fo well*, as that which has been the long admired *native* of the foil.

† The following accurate valuation of two pieces of coppice wood in my neighbourhood, on both of which *referves* had been left in the manner I have advifed, came to me too late for infertion in its proper place; but as I have received it from a very well informed gentleman, who has dealt largely in woods, and find it contains fuch

important

plants but lately fingled out, are now beginning to fhew the great advantage of being allowed a fufficient fpace for their growth, and a free circulation

---

important information on the fubject, as ftrongly corroborates what I have before advanced, I fhall take the liberty of inferting it here.

Value of one acre of coppice wood, in which there are now ftanding one hundred Oak referves, of 56 years growth:

	£.	s.	d.
The referves at £1 : 5s. each on an average,	125	0	0
The younger growth of the coppice, now in its 34th year very thin, but the poles good, as remaining after many of an inferior fort had been taken away at different times,	50	0	0
Total value of the acre, —	£175	0	0

Or five pounds per annum, for 35 years, viz. fince the laft fall.

circulation of air; whilſt the *fine heads* they are forming, and the ſmoothneſs and brightneſs of their *bark* prove, what numbers may be thinned out of a coppice, (if done gradually) without the leaſt danger to the remainder from want of ſufficient ſhelter.

The growth of the *Aſh* in theſe woods, is generally ſomewhat more than that of the *Oak*, yet does not exceed it as much in proportion, as from the nature of the two trees, it might be ſuppoſed

---

Value of half an acre of coppice wood, on which there are now ſtanding eighty reſerves, of 56 years growth, ſome from the Acorn, but moſt from the old ſtools:

Theſe reſerves are now worth each £1: 10s.
on an average, — — £120 0 0

The value of the acre at the ſame rate, would be £240—There is at preſent little value in the underwood, as the beſt has been moſtly taken away from time to time, but by good information it may have amounted to £50 in the whole, which brings the value of the acre thus managed, to £290, or nearly £5: 4s. per annum for the 56 years it has ſtood.

supposed to do; but the *Birch* of the same age, is often more than a *fifth* grosser than the best *Ash* or *Oak* in its vicinity, and of surprising height.—So, that as the *bark* is worth half what *Oak bark* sells for, and the timber is excellent for almost every rural purpose, it will be found highly advantageous to cultivate this tree in all our *coppices*, as it ensures an immediate profit, with little or no injury to any other tree, from the peculiar lightness and flexibility of its branches; which just preserve a proper place during their standing, to receive the undamaged branches of the more *valuable* trees after the fall of the *Birch*.

In a meadow below the woods is an *Ash* from an *old root* of 31 years growth in 1794, which now measures 6 feet 6 inches round within a foot of the ground, and 5 feet 8 inches at 5 feet high; this stands near the river, and not far from the great *Ash* tree I mentioned before, as growing three parts in water.

We might naturally attribute the size of the above to the nature of the soil, which seems peculiarly adapted to the *Ash*, but that its dimensions are fully equalled by another *Ash* tree in the same demesne, though of a still *younger* standing, and growing in a *dry* soil, on a high situation.

This in the year 1771, could not have exceeded six inches in circumference, having at that time narrowly escaped being cut down by a labourer for the handle of his shovel; it now measures in its twenty-third year from that date, seven feet eight inches round at a foot high, five feet eight inches at five feet, continues nearly of that size for *several* feet more, and then branches into a very large head.

On deducting six inches, the greatest circumference of this tree in 1771, from the average of its present dimensions, viz. eighty inches, we shall have seventy-four inches for
twenty-

twenty-three years growth, or nearly three inches and a quarter for every year*.

It would be superfluous to add more to the foregoing proofs, on what a sure foundation the

Planter

---

* On comparing these several measurements with some which are communicated to the *Bath and West of England Society*, by a very ingenious correspondent in *Norfolk*, we shall have ample reason to be satisfied with the *growth* of our timber in this kingdom.

We find by his account, that *Black Poplar* planted in 1746, measured after forty-four years growth, viz. in 1790, but six feet six inches round at five feet from the ground.—Another sort of Poplar or Abele, planted in large truncheons in 1760, after *thirty* years standing, were not quite six feet in circumference.

Ash planted at eight feet high in 1760, were but from three feet eight inches to four feet round, and *Oak* which were transplanted in 1764, and were then about three feet high, measured at five feet from the ground, from one foot six inches to two feet four inches at the very most, which on an average, does not amount to two-thirds of the growth of my Oak before mentioned, tho' nearly of the same age.

Planter may build the moſt ſanguine expectations of ſucceſs —I could adduce many others of a ſimilar nature, and on the moſt reſpectable authority; but as I had premiſed in the outſet of this little work, that I would offer few or none, which had not *grown*, in ſome meaſure under my immediate *obſervation*, I have choſen to confine myſelf almoſt literally to my own grounds.

I flatter myſelf however, that the enquiry I have ſet on foot on the growth of timber, and the more perfect management of woods, will be followed up by others, who, with an equal love of trees, and perhaps greater experience, may poſſeſs more leiſure time than I had, to devote to this equally uſeful and intereſting purſuit, the avowed favourite indeed of ſome of the greateſt and wiſeſt of every *clime* and *age*; and yet of none more perhaps, than the *preſent*.

The improvements by *plantation* which have been made in this kingdom and in England,

and

and ſtill more, as I am credibly informed, in *Scotland*, within theſe few years, afford manifeſt proofs of the liberality and ſpirit of the individuals who have undertaken them, as they will do infinite credit hereafter to the age in which they were carried into execution.

Nor is this ſpirit of improvement confined to individuals; the exertions of the ſeveral *ſocieties* for the advancement of agriculture, manufactures and fine arts, have been attended with every poſſible ſucceſs which could have been hoped for, from their reſpective inſtitutions.—In aid of the Society for the Encouragement of Arts, &c. in London, we find, that a diſtinct Board of Agriculture has been formed under the higheſt patronage; together with a ſociety for the improvement of Britiſh wool; and commiſſioners have been appointed to examine into the ſtate of the woods and foreſts belonging to the Crown, who appear by their conduct, to have very much at heart, a faithful diſcharge of the duties of their office.

Many

Many other communities for the advancement of the science of rural œconomics, arts and manufactures, have been set on foot in different parts of the kingdom; those of *Bath* and *Manchester* have not only gained singular reputation by their ingenious publications, but have already proved of the greatest utility to the cause in which they have engaged.

We have as yet formed few societies in this kingdom as correspondent with that of DUBLIN, but the *parent* society has not been *idle*.

The following extracts from their proceedings, will not only evince the truth of this assertion, but will serve to mark the *progressive* state of improvement which *Ireland* enjoyed for some years past, till the unhappy situation of affairs on the continent, and some disagreeable circumstances in consequence at home, produced a sort of alarm thro' the kingdom, from which tho' happily much recovered, we cannot as yet say we are perfectly free.

BOUNTIES

PAID BY THE

DUBLIN SOCIETY,

From the YEAR 1783, to the YEAR 1791,

On the Propagation and Sale of

TIMBER TREES,

And Number of Trees Sold.

	PROPAGATED and Sold.	BOUNTY paid on the Sale.		
		£.	s.	d.
In 1784	65,158 —	50	0	0
1785	1,205,000 —	185	0	0
1786	1,506,553 —	217	14	0
1789	1,359,280 —	241	7	0
1790	3,763,500 —	526	10	0

It also appears from the minutes of the Society, that in the year 1784, the total number of acres under every improvement, which

was

was at that time the object of their bounty, amounted to ninety only, and that the sum of money expended in various agricultural premiums in that year, did not not exceed *four hundred and sixty-eight pounds.*

In 1785, The number of acres, for the improvement of which any Claims were made, amounted to - - 272

 Money expended in bounties and premiums, - £1052

In 1786, Number of acres claimed for, 3183

 Money expended in bounties and premiums, - £3430

In 1787, Number of acres claimed for, 5113

 Money expended by the society in consequence, - £4168

And

And in 1788, there were Claimants for
   the improvement of 9664
  acres,
  For which the Society paid
  in bounties and premiums
     £4876

I have already mentioned the advantages arifing from the act of parliament, which confers upon the tenant a power of fencing up for his own ufe, under certain reftrictions, fuch tracts of woodland on his farm as have been left by the landlord for a certain number of years expofed to cattle; the *Society* have added a further encouragement to tenants holding on determinable leafes, by granting a bounty of forty fhillings on every acre thus fenced up for coppice wood; and it is worth obferving, that in addition to the great number of trees which muft be annually planted on fmaller enclofures, thofe which have been put out by perfons claiming a bounty for plantations not lefs than ten acres in extent, have amounted on an average, for fome years paft, to five hundred thoufand in each year.

For some years indeed previous to 1784, the Dublin Society had turned their attention so much to *Arts and Manufactures*, as in a great measure to lose sight of the principal object of their formation; but the above statement of facts fully proves, that since that period, their exertions in the advancement of Agriculture and Planting have been so strenuous, and attended with such success, that this Society as an Institution for the improvement of Husbandry, may with great justice claim the distinction not only of being the *earliest* of its kind in Europe, but perhaps at this time the most considerable and comprehensive in its views.

Amongst many other instances of liberal expenditure to promote this great national object, a Repository has been provided for the reception of Specimens of every useful Implement of Agriculture, which can be procured from England, Flanders, or any other country, which makes the least pretensions to good Husbandry. This excellent establishment is daily improving under the direction of the Committee of Agriculture chosen by ballot from the whole Society these
Gentlemen

Gentlemen* have been neither sparing of application or expence to render the collection of Implements as perfect as possible; they have also carried their attention to the other useful Arts, by the addition of a large Apartment furnished with *Models* of the best constructed Machines, in various branches of Manufactures, &c; they have formed a considerable Library of valuable Books, connected in general with all the Arts and Sciences, but more particularly with *Rural œconomicks, Botany* and *Natural History*.

---

* PRESENT MEMBERS,

Rt. Hon. John Foster, Speaker of H. Commons,
Morgan Crofton, Esq.
Thomas Burgh, Esq.
John Leigh, Esq.
Arthur Maguire, Esq.
Lodge Morres, Esq.
Thomas Fitzgerald, Esq.
Samuel Hayes, Esq.
Cornelius Bolton, Esq.
Nicholas Westby, Esq.
Richard Reynell, Esq.
Right Rev. the Bishop of Kilmore.
Major General Eustace.
Sir William Gleadowe Newcomen, Bart.
Sir Lucius O'Brien, Bart.

A new range of buildings are now conſtructing defigned partly for the reception of a Cabinet of Mineralogy*, and partly for more convenient School-rooms than the Society now poffefs, for the purpofe of giving Inſtructions gratis in *Figure Drawing*, *Ornament* and *Architecture*, to fuch youths as manifeſt an early genius for the Arts, but whofe parents are not in fufficient circumſtances to afford them inſtruction adequate to their wifhes.

A room will alfo be adapted to the purpofe of giving practical Lectures on Chymiſtry, and a confiderable fum of money is appropriated for providing and maintaining a Garden for the Improvement of the Science of *Botany* and *Planting*.

When

---

* This Cabinet, which is well known on the Continent by the name of the Lefkean Mufeum, and has been mentioned in feveral publications, in terms of the higheſt approbation, was purchafed for the Dublin Society in the year 1792, for £1250. by that excellent Mineralogiſt Richard Kirwan, Efq. under whofe infpection the collection is to be arranged.

When thefe arrangements are completed, which may be expected to take place before the end of the year 1794, we may venture to fay, that the general Eftablifhment will not only exceed any Inftitution of a fimilar nature which has hitherto been carried into execution, but will nearly equal an *Ideal Scheme* formed upon the like plan by the patriotic SULLY, and offered by that judicious and enterprifing Minifter to the confideration of HENRY the Fourth of France, as worthy of being adopted by that great Monarch, fo indefatigable in every purfuit, which could promote the welfare and happinefs of his People.

THE END.

Index

A

Abbey Leix, Queen's County, 153–154
abele, speed of growth, 179
Abercorn, Marquis of, 155
Act of Union (1800), VII
Acton, Thomas, 121
alder, 86
Anderson (James), 4
apple, 32–34
arbutus, 127, 130
Arklow, Co. Wicklow, 118
Arles, Queen's County, 147–148
Ascendancy *see* Protestant landed gentry
ash, 26, 38, 86
  perfection of form, 147
  specimen of, 120, 123, 130, 132, 134–135, 137–140, 142, 145–151
  speed of growth, 176–179
Ashbrook, Lord, 151
Author's own observations *see* Hayes
Avondale, Co. Wicklow, V–VI, VII, XVI, XVII–XVIII, 165, 169–180
  Gothick woodhouse at, XII
Avonmore River, V, 120

B

Bagot oak (walking stick), 125
Bagshot (Surrey), 52–53
Ballyarthur, Co. Wicklow, 83–85
Ballybeg, Co. Wicklow, 116–118
Ballycavan, Queen's County, 65
Ballygannon, Co. Wicklow, 131
Bank of Ireland, X
bark,
  bounty on imports, 108
  value of in birch, 177
baskets, 87 (Plate III)
Bath and West of England Society, 170, 179
Bath Society, 78, 82
bay tree, specimen of, 133
beech, XV, XVI–XVII, 19–22, 48, 50–51
  at Avondale, VI, XVII
  longevity of, 170
  progress of, 169–170
  propagation from Shelton, 118
  sites for, 171
  specimen of, 118
  suitability for Ireland, XVII
Bellevue, Co. Galway, 162–163
Bellevue, Co. Wicklow, 154
Beresford, John, X
Bernard, Thomas, 139
birch, 48–51, 86

speed of growth, 176–177
Birchland oak, 126
birds, preventing, 8
black poplar, speed of growth, 179
botanical garden, 188
botanical varieties *see* Collon
bounties paid by Dublin Society, 183–185
Boutcher (William), vi, 6, 10, 19, 25, 26, 44, 66
Bray, Co. Wicklow, 133
British Navy, XV
Burgh, William, 127
Bury, Charles, 139

C

cabinet for mineralogy, 188
cacagee (Irish cider apple), 33
Cahirnane, Co. Cork, 158–159
Caldbeck, William, 143
Carhampton, Co. Dublin, 133
Carrickglass, Co. Longford, 163–164
Carton, Co. Kildare, 136–137
Castledurrow, Queen's County, 151
Castletown, King's County, 139
cedar of Lebanon, 50
Charlemont, Earl of, 155
Charles II, King of England, XIV, 111
Charleville, King's County, 139
chemistry, lectures on, 188
cherry, 38
chestnut of the hundred horses, 126
chestnut, Spanish, 9, 16–17, 38, 48, 50–51, 53
 age of, 121
 avenue of, 121
 qualities of, 162
 specimen of, 162–163
chestnut, sweet, XVII
Chritchley, James, 93
Clarecastle, Co. Galway, 137
Clermont, Lord, XIII
College Green, Dublin, VII, X
Claude Lorraine, 132
Collon, Co. Louth, wealth of species, 173
Committee of Agriculture, 186–187
composition, Forsyth's, 70, 99–104
Conolly, Thomas, 135
Conyngham, Mr, 155
Coolattin, Co. Wicklow, XVI, 116
coppice oak, value of, 175
coppice thinnings, 86–89
coppices,
 collection of broomsticks, 173

timber from, 90–94
Courtown, Earl of, 145–146
Cowthorpe oak, 127, 137, 148
crab tree, 2, 32–3
crooked wood, advantage of, 88–89
Crown Commissioners for Woods, 181
Cumberland, Duke of, 52–53
Cunninghame, General, 128, 155
Curraghmore, Co. Waterford, 141
Custom House, Dublin, X

D

de Vesci, Lord, 153
Deer Park, Shillelagh, 114
Desart, Earl of, 138
digging, 12–13
Donane Colliery, 115
Donirey ash, 137
dotting, disadvantage of, 44–45
Down, County, XIII
Downshire, Marquis of, 155
dryads, slighting, 157
drying, risks of, 23
Dublin Society (later Royal Dublin Society), XII, v, ix, 182, 183–9
Dublin, Archbishop of, 92–93
Dublin, County, XVI, 107
Ducie chestnut, 127

Dunganstown, Co. Wicklow, 121, 123
Dunmore, Queen's County, 153

E

Edgar's nursery (Dublin), 26
Edwards, John, 131
elm, 38
  finest specimen in the world, 135–136
  specimen of, 118, 133, 134, 136–7, 138, 150, 151, 162
Ely, Earl of, 133
Emo Park, Queen's County, 149–150
England's Improvement, 30
English Garden, 45
Esdall, William, XI–XII
Etna, Mount, 126
Evelyn, John, XIV–XV, 22–23, 90, 127, 155
evergreens, transplanting, 27
exposed situations, 28–31

F

Fairwood Park, Co. Wicklow, 79–82, 116
felling, time for, 160–161
fencing against cattle, 185
fertility in nursery, 18

Fitzwilliam, Earl, XI, 80, 113–114
Flannel Hall, Rathdrum, 113
forest trees, selecting, 38, 48
forges, iron, 106, 110–114
forked oak, value of, 81–82
Fornace *see* Furness
Forsyth (William), 70, 99–104
Fortescue (James), XIII, vi, 6, 17, 28, 40, 58–69, 64, 128, 143
Foster, John, IX, X, XII, 155, 173
Four Courts, Dublin, X
French Revolution, VIII
frost, preventing, 8
fruit tree walk, 36–37
funeral tree, 139
Furness (Fornace), Co. Kildare, yew at, 145

G

Gandon, James, X
garden for studying botany, 188
Glendalough, Co. Wicklow, 92–93
yew at, 145
Glendelough (*see* Glendalough, Co. Wicklow)
Gloster (King's County), 65
Gormanstown, Co. Meath, 152–153
ground for sowing, 10–15

H

Hamel, M. de, 159–160
handles for pitchforks, 86
Hardy, Mr (inspector of claims), 137
Hayes, Samuel, 180
admiration for naturalised trees, VI, XVII
as artist, 105
authorship of illustrations, XI
birth, V
builds Avondale, V–VI
career as barrister, VI
career in Irish House of Commons, VI
colonel of Volunteers, VI
death, VII
leads fashion for planting, VII
Lieutenant-Colonel of militia, VII
lists of champion trees, XVI
memorial slab at Rathdrum Church, XVIII–XIX
publishes *Practical Treatise*, VII, XI
service as Colonel of Wicklow Foresters, VI
skill as amateur architect, VI, IX, X
success as author, XI
views on planting techniques, XV–XVI
Hayesville *see* Avondale

hazel, 39, 87
hedging, 2–5
Henry IV, King of France, 189
Henry VIII, King of England, 90
Herbert, R. T., 158
Herefordshire, 34
Hillbrook, Co. Wicklow, 118
hill tops, 49
Hints on Planting (Fortescue), 1, 28–30, 128
hoe, planting, 41
Hoey, William, 121–123
holes, planting, 40–41, 47, 54–56
holly, 50
  silver, 131
  specimen of, 143
Holt Forest oak, 127
hops, 150
horse chestnut, specimen of, 153
House of Commons, Irish, VII, VIII
Huleat, Rev. Mr, 140
hurdles for sheep, 87 (Plate III)

I

ilex, specimen of, 132
Ireland
  alarm in, 182
  progress in, 182
Irish oak, preference for, 110

Irish Tree Society, XIV

J

juniper, 50
Justice, James, XIII, vi, 6

K

Kaims, Lord, 3, 26
Kennedy, vi, 10, 13, 17, 53
Kennity (Kinnity), King's County, 139
Kerles, Mr of Ross, 34–36
Kildare, County, 135
Kilkenny, County, 138
Killaloe, Bishop of, 135
Killarney, Co. Cork, 158–159
Killarney, Lake of, Co. Cork, 143
Kilmacurragh (Westaston), Co. Wicklow, 121
Kilmurry, King's County, 140
Kilruddery, Co. Wicklow, 132
King, Thomas, 121
King's College, Cambridge, 110
Kinnity see Kennity

L

laburnam, 39
landlords, absentee, 113
Langley oak (Hampshire), 82
Laois *see* Queen's County

larch, 48, 50–51, 139
  transplanting, 28
laurel, specimen of, 131
Laurence, Walter, 162–163
law, affecting tenants, 93
Leinster, Duke of, 136–137
Leix
  great ash of, XII, 105 (illustration by S. H.), 148–149
  small tree of, 149
Leixlip, Co. Dublin, 135
library, 187
lime, specimen of, 150
liming, 49
Lorraine, Claude, 132
Loughlinstown, Co. Dublin, 133
Lucombe Oak, 172
Luttrelstown, Co. Dublin, 133

M

machine for transplanting, 42–46
Maryborough (Portlaoise), VI
Mason (poet), 45
mice, preventing, 9–10
Middleton oak, 126
Miller (Philip), XIII, vi, 6, 26
Milton, John, 154
models of machines, 187
Mount Usher (Co. Wicklow), XVI, 64, 124
Mountjoy, Lord, 155

Mount-Kennedy, Co. Wicklow, 127, 130
Moyne, Queen's County, 152
mummy wax, 100–104
myrtle, 123

N

Newcomen, Sir William, 163–164
Newry, Co. Down, XIII
Nore, River, 153
nursery, 5–18

O

oak, 16, 38, 48, 51
  at Powerscourt, 132
  at Shillelagh and Coolattin, XVI
  disadvantages of foreign species, 173
  exports, 110
  felling, 160–161
  Milltown, 123–4
  sessile, VI
  specimen of, 119, 138, 142, 151, 153, 158, 161–162, 172–176
  specimens of (English), 125–7
  speed of growth, 117–118
  thinnings, 88
  transplanting, 26–27, 169
  value of, 73–85, 156

Old Connaught, Co. Dublin, 133
Old Court, Co. Wicklow, 131

P

Parliament
　Irish, VII–VIII
　British, VIII
Parliament oak, 126
Parnell, Sir John, IX, 155
pear, 34
Pery, 34–35
Petrie oak, 127
Pinus sylvestris see Scots pine
plantations,
　management of, 69
　selection of tree species for, 171
planter, expectations for, 180
planting
　improvements, 180–182
　techniques, 23, 38, 48, 56–57
　the favourite occupation, 180
　time for, 25–27
ploughing, 49
poor, education of, 154
Pope, Alexander, 34
Portarlington, Earl of, 149
Portland, Duke of, 47–52, 125–126
Portland oak (walking stick), 125
Portuguese laurel,
　specimen of, 131
Poussin (Gaspar), 132
Powerscourt, Co. Wicklow, 132
Powerscourt, Lord, 132
Practical Treatise on Planting
　engravings in, XI–XII
　authorship of illustrations, XI–XII
pricking out, 15–16
Protestant landed gentry, VII
pruning
　in nursery, 18–22
　dangers of, 71

Q

Queen's County (Laois), 107, 147–148, 151, 153
quick hedge (whitethorn), 2–5

R

Rathdrum, Co. Wicklow, 113, 119, 121
Rathdrum Church, Co, Wicklow, XVIII
Rathdrum, hall (Co. Wicklow), 80
Rathfarnham, Co. Dublin, 133
Rathleague, Queen's County, 151
Rebellion of 1798, VIII
repository of specimens, 186
reserves, need for, 76, 79

ridings (rides), 49
Robinson, Mr (Scottish engineer), 42–45
Rockingham, Marquis of, 112
root
　damage, 23–24
　pruning, 21
Ross (Herefordshire), 34
Rossana, Co. Wicklow, 123–124, 154
rotten boroughs, VIII
Royal Irish Academy, XIII
rustic woodwork, 86–87 (Plate II)

S

sallow *see* willow
school in ash tree, 137
Scot, Mr (wood agent), 114
Scotch fir *see* Scots pine
Scots pine, 7, 27, 57–63, 118, 139, 167
　and sycamore, 134
　Co. Dublin, 133–134
　ornamental qualities of, 150, 151
　specimen of, 131, 150
Shanley, Mr, 165–166
Shannon, Earl of, 155
shears for pruning, 71
shelter, importance of, 1–2, 28, 42
Shelton Abbey, Co. Wicklow, XVI, 118

Shillela (Shillelagh), Co. Wicklow, XVI, 79–82, 110–118, 121
Shillelagh *see* Shillela
Shire oak, 126
shoots,
　potential for, 76, 82, 116–117
　trees from, 92–98 (illustration)
shrubs for plantations, 38–39
silver fir, 48, 53, 63–65, 139
　at Avondale, XVII
　specimen of, 124
single species, danger of, 40
Sisson, Mr (master builder), 81–82, 112
Smith, 30
Smyth, Sir Skeffington, 130
Society for the Improvement of the Arts, 181
soil
　dry, 47–52
　fertility, 42
　shallow moory, 57–67
　shallow rocky, 53–67
Some Hints on Planting, XIII
South, Mr, 82, 170
sowing directly, 6, 51–2, 57
specimen trees, 64–65
Speechley (William), 20–21, 24, 47–52
Spenser, Edmund, 147
spruce

common, 63, 65–67
Cornish, 165
specimen of, 138–139
weeping, 165–166
St Wolstan's, Co. Kildare, 135
Stafford, Earl of *see* Strafford, Earl of
Staples, Sir Robert, 153
stone pine, specimen of, 131
Strafford, Earl of, 80, 111, 116
straight lines, danger of, 38
strawberry tree, 127, 130
Stubber, Ralph, 152
Sully, 189
Swilcar oak, 125
sycamore, VI, XVII
and Scots pine, 134
largest specimen of, 121
Sylva, XIV–XV, 155
Symes, Colonel, 83–85
Symes, Mrs, 118
Symes, Rev. Mr, 116

T

table from ash, 120
tenants
act for encouraging, 185
fairness to, 113
for life, 91–93
law affecting, 93
thinning, need for, 66
Tighe, Mrs, 123–124
timber trees
from coppices, 90–94
propagation and sale of, 183
timber, waste of, 106
Tiny Park, Co. Wicklow, 130
transplanting, 19–28
large trees, 42–45
tree longevity, 143
tree measuring, 129
tree vandalism, 145
trees
champion, XVI
ethnic cleansing of, XVII
grants from Dublin Society, XIII
management of, 105–8
naturalised in Ireland, VI, XVI–XVII
planting distance, 167–168
speed of growth, 143, 158–179
value of, 111–115, 119–121, 156, 168–169
trench-plowing, 28–29
tulip tree, 50
turkey oak, 173
turner oak, 174
Tyrol, 32

V

Virginian julip-tree *see* tulip tree

W

Wainwright, Mr, 114

walnut, VI, 9, 16–17, 38
Walpole, Horace, 116
Warwickshire, 77
waste by tenants, 91–93
Waterford, Marquis of, 141, 155
Welbeck (Abbey), 20–21, 24, 47–52
Westaston *see* Kilmacurragh
Westminster Abbey, London, 110
Westminster Hall, London, 110
Wexford, County, 145–146
Weymouth Pine, XVI, 48, 64–65, 166, 169
whitethorn, 39
  specimens of, 152
Wicklow, County, V, XVI, 27, 64, 107
Wicklow Foresters, Volunteer regiment of, VI
Wicklow, Viscount, 118
William III, King of England, 91
willow, 87
Windsor beech, 170
Wood, Laurence, 111
Wyatt, James, VI

Y

Yelverton, Chief Baron, 143
yew, 50

  at Fornace (Furness), Co. Kildare 145
  at Glendalough 144–145
  line of, 122–123
  perfect form, 122–123
  specimen of, 145, 150
Young, Arthur, 112–113, 128

Note: Irish estates and demesnes in bold type.